PERUVIAN JOURNAL

LETTERS OF A GRINGO PRIEST

by

Charles O'Neill Conroy

Painting by Helen Parsons Shephard

Fr. Charles O'Neill Conroy

PERUVIAN JOURNAL

Letters of a Gringo Priest

by

Charles O'Neill Conroy

FOREWORD

† G. Emmett Carter
Bishop of London

INTRODUCTION

Walter O'Hearn

PALM PUBLISHERS,
MONTREAL

1966

Palm Publishers
1949 - 55th Avenue Dorval,
Montreal, P.Q., Canada.

Printed in Canada — Harpell Press, St. Anne de Bellevue, P.Q.

INDEX OF PICTURES

Fronticepiece: Painting of Father Conroy by
Helen Parsons Shepherd

DEDICATION

To the memory of Sister Mary Dorothy Carroll and Sister Mary Aquin English of the Order of Our Lady of Mercy and of Sister Mary De Chantal Krysinski of the Sisters of the Holy Family of Nazareth, who died with Father Conroy;

To all those who worked with him in establishing and carrying on the mission in Monsefú;

To all those other priests and nuns, whether from Canada, the United States, Ireland or elsewhere, who have engaged themselves, as he did, in extending help to the hard-pressed clergy of Latin America and in contributing to the material and spiritual enlightenment of its people.

The material in this book is taken from letters to Father Conroy's family, together with monthly letters which he wrote for 'The Monitor', the St. John's, Newfoundland, diocesan paper.

FOREWORD

Of the many, many mysteries that God reserves to Himself perhaps none is more baffling than the mystery of life and death. In our ignorance and narrowness of view we decide for ourselves who is called to live and who is called to die. We wonder at the choice of survivors and at the length of days given to some, while others have fulfilled their span of years before we are truly aware of their presence.

Apparently the secret lies in some hidden qualitative process in God. And while we conjecture about the good which might have been done by some men, their very goodness leads us to suspect that their mission was fulfilled even though so much more appeared to remain. Because, if we stop to think about it, though we live a thousand years there would still be everything to do in this evolving world of ours.

These words I write tonight, roughly half a year since I saw Father Charles Conroy in vibrant health on one day and heard the news of his death so soon after that it seemed like the next day. My suggestion on the subject is not the immediate fruit of the vine of this particular disaster. My first reaction was of such shock, such unbelieving impossibility, that I have not been able, until recently, to set my thoughts in order.

Tonight, also, I have read Father Conroy's letters. Already there is a little light in the fact that he should have felt called to place so many thoughts on paper. He seemed to have been driven by compulsion to leave us a legacy of his extraordinary perception of the missionary problem, in particular, the problem of Perú. Indeed the last time I saw him — literally — he had his portable typewriter with him. He had brought some straw mats, the industry of Monsefú which he had promoted, to my hotel room so that I might purchase them and take them home as souvenirs. In order that he would lose no time he had brought his typewriter and was banging away at it on the latest assemblage of thoughts concerning Perú which had crossed, or shall I say, which had penetrated his mind. I saw him again as I was escorted to the plane at the airport. He was still taking time out to type.

Authors have written of the "Secret" of the Curé of Ars and of other saints. I do not pretend to know the secret of Father Charles Conroy. It is true that I have known him practically all of his life, even if not all of mine. And the only word which can truly qualify him is a word which is frequently misused and must be taken in its etymological sense. It is the word "extraordinary". In truth, he never seemed to follow the quite ordinary path.

The first time I met him was when he was a young student. He burst into my office one day highly intent upon joining the Catholic Worker Movement. In our days of protests, of fringe groups and social reaction of all kinds, we would hardly term such an ambition in a young man as extraordinary. But remember that this was a lot closer to 1946 than to 1966. The only thing that slowed Charlie down and kept him from heading for the slums of New York was a deep sense that God had something else in store for him. How right he was.

As is frequently the case, we find some of the answer in a man's own writings. In this case, strangely enough, we find it right at the beginning of his letters. As the reader can see, he began his missionary odyssey in November 1960. The second letter is dated from La Paz, Bolivia, November 8. In the fourth sentence of this letter he informs us . . . "but now I could take on all of Bolivia, with all its problems. Maybe it is what Captain Cousteau, who invented the aqualung, described as *ivresse des profondeurs*, only this is the heights." He said it but he didn't know what he was saying. For here *is* the man himself. *Ivresse des hauteurs*, indeed! Father Conroy was a dweller on the heights.

Although I never lost sight of Charlie and his family completely, he passed out of my immediate ken when he went to Latin America in 1960. At that time I was still working in Montreal and the affairs of Latin America were fairly remote. I had no idea how our paths were going to cross again.

In 1962 a wise providence, kind or otherwise, guided my destiny to the episcopacy when I was appointed Auxiliary Bishop to Bishop John C. Cody. As Father Conroy's letters indicate, it was Archbishop Skinner and Bishop Cody who teamed together to send the first Canadian group to this part of Perú. They adopted the parish of Monsefú as a beginning. Father Charles Conroy and Father Richard Morse went together to establish the beachhead.

I arrived in the Diocese of London in the winter of 1962. I found Bishop Cody fresh from his visit to the mission at Monsefú. He had much to say and was high in his praise of the whole team, sparing no compliment for the work of Father Conroy. He informed me without hesitation that it was his strong wish that I visit the mission the following winter. I was more than happy to acquiesce.

It was in this way that in the winter of 1963 I found myself with Father Lawrence Paré seated at table with the Apostolic Nuncio in Lima listening to his enthusiasm about what he called marriage of the North American mentality with that of the South. The London group had then separated from the Newfoundland group, but only the space of a very few miles — and not at all psychologically and apostolically.

In fact, the next day, upon my arrival at the airport in Chiclayo, I found out that you needed a program to tell the London effort from the Newfoundland endeavour.

So it was that again I could see and observe this strange young man. He lacked none of the human qualities and was witty and joyful, although, at times, the *ivresse des hauteurs* had him manifestly in its grasp.

The story of his becoming Mayor of Monsefú, of the hold he had over this simple but difficult people, of the atmosphere of the village when one entered it with him, to the inevitable cries of "Padre Carlos!"; all of these things are written in the letters or behind them. The reader must see for himself and judge for himself. All I can do is to touch the surface as an introduction to a profound personality.

Two years elapsed before my subsequent return to Perú. Much had happened. Among other things Bishop Cody was dead and I had succeeded him. I was doing my best to follow in the footsteps of Archbishop Skinner and Bishop Cody and had raised the sights of our mission. We now had five priests planned for Perú. Four of them were already there and these, combined with the three Newfoundlanders, formed a formidable and effective group.

I see Father Conroy still, sitting on the beach, (the Newfoundlanders' substitute for the daily siesta,) reading a profound tome on social progress or a report from the latest French sociologist, while the rest of us were half asleep.

He began to speak to me of the problem of Latin America and its profound significance and conditions. I listened with some awe. Nor was he satisfied with what could be done with the particular region in which we worked. All of Perú was his worry. Indeed, to use his own words, he "could have taken on all of Bolivia" and you can add the rest of Latin America.

He delved into some of his theories and suggested to me what the Canadian Bishops might be prepared to do to coordinate and strengthen their Latin American effort. I made notes, but I felt he was the man to present the case and could do so much better, certainly with more conviction and passion than I could. I had already referred him to our Latin American Commission and was preparing to put him in contact with it when God spun the wheel.

One morning, a few weeks after my return from Perú, I entered my office in London and read my mail. There was a letter from Archbishop Skinner which interested and intrigued me. The Archbishop informed me that he was posting Father Conroy for further training in the field of religious education and that he would be a member of our first class at our new Centre for Religious Education, The Divine Word, in London, Ontario. I walked into the office of the Director of the Centre and said, "Father O'Flaherty, we have a tiger by the tail. Father Charlie Conroy will be with us in September. We had better be good." Minutes after, the telephone rang with the incredible tidings. Father Conroy was dead.

I leave the reader to the perusal of these letters. They are dramatic, appealing, easy reading. But before you begin, let me remind you of a few things. I have seen pictures of the men of Monsefú as they carried the body of Father Conroy. Their faces mirrored their almost unbearable grief and their sense of loss and bewilderment. I have seen pictures of the highway leading to the airport in St. John's, Newfoundland, choked with traffic on a cold and stormy March day as the people awaited the arrival of the aircraft bearing the mortal remains of Father Conroy, simply in order to pay homage to him. I have seen pictures of the massed assembly in the Cathedral at St. John's on the day of the formal funeral service.

There was something in this man which stirred his fellows. It is almost sacrilegious and clearly impossible to put it into words. But, one has to feel that complete devotion to the welfare of others sets up a mysterious wave which knows no obstacles and which defies time and place, language and race.

Shortly after his arrival in Monsefú, Father Conroy talks about a train-car collision in which many persons were killed. He says, "There was blood on our hands as we administered the sacrament of Extreme Unction."

There was blood on the highway that night when Father Conroy died on the road which runs from Trujillo to Monsefú. The blood of a young Canadian priest which, since his earliest youth, had flowed, apparently, only in one direction. Towards others.

† G. Emmett Carter,
Bishop of London, Ont.

The Peruvian authorities, to commemorate the contribution made by the late Fr. Conroy, named the thoroughfare at Monsefú in his honour. Above, we see the granite block, in the centre of the boulevard with 36 feet wide driveways on either side, standing to-day as a reminder of his work.

INTRODUCTION

by Walter O'Hearn

Early in the evening of Tuesday, March 1st, 1966, a small European micro-bus was moving north on the Pan American Highway in the direction of Chiclayo, the principal city of northern Peru. It belonged to the Convent of the Sisters of Mercy in Monsefú, which is a town of some 12,000 people, about 10 miles from Chiclayo. In it were four Canadian nuns from Monsefú and two sisters of an American order, who were serving in the mountain parish of Santa Cruz and were on a visit to the Mercy sisters. The driver was the parish priest of Monsefú, Father Charles Conroy, also a Canadian.

A light truck was speeding south on the same highway. It had been stolen some days before from its owners in Chimbote, about 180 miles south of Chiclayo. It had been recovered by the police, and the driver and his brother had been sent to Chiclayo to bring it back to Chimbote. Now they were in haste to get home. Ahead of them a small car was proceeding sedately in the same direction. Rapidly they overtook it, speeded up still more as they swung out suddenly to pass it, and at once crashed head-on into the micro-bus.

The two occupants of the truck received only minor injuries but the smaller vehicle was practically demolished. Sister M. Aquin, of the Mercy Order, was killed almost instantly; the Superior of the Convent, Sister M. Dorothy, died after lingering unconscious for nearly two weeks; Sister M. de Chantal, from Santa Cruz, died about the same time; her companion, Sister M. Charlotte, was brought home eventually for a long convalescence in the United States; Sisters M. Immaculata and M. Carmelita recovered after several months in hospital in Lima and returned to Monsefú. Father Conroy died, without regaining consciousness, as he was being carried into the hospital in Chiclayo.

To trace the events that led to this catastrophe, we must go back at least to 1959. In November of that year, in response to an appeal from Pope John XXIII, an Inter-American Episcopal Conference was held in Washington. Representatives of the

Hierarchies of Latin America, the United States and Canada, met to discuss the problems of the Catholic Church, with particular reference to the Latin American countries. One of their principal difficulties was acknowledged to be that of finding enough young men of suitable character and education to enter the priestly vocation. The American and Canadian bishops promised to do whatever they could to help in providing both men and money. Archbishop Skinner of St. John's, Newfoundland, and Bishop Cody of London, Ontario, each undertook to send one man without delay. They agreed that the two priests whom they were sending should embark on this adventure together. Archbishop Skinner's choice for the pioneering assignment was a young priest attached to the staff of the Cathedral in St. John's, Father Conroy.

Charles O'Neill Conroy was born in St. John's on April 3rd, 1928. His father, a rising young lawyer, died when the boy was barely three years old and his sister only a few months. His mother, left with two children to support, herself entered a law office, qualified for the bar and successfully practised law for the next ten years.

Charlie's early education was received from the Irish Christian brothers at St. Bonaventure's College in St. John's. When he was thirteen he was sent to Montreal to attend high school at Loyola College. Two years later his sister was sent to school at the Sacred Heart Convent in Montreal and the following year his mother re-married, gave up her law practice and moved to Montreal, which was thenceforth the family home.

While still a schoolboy, Charlie decided that he had a vocation for the priesthood. His mind once made up, he was impatient to get started at once on his training. After only one year of university work at Loyola, he insisted that to proceed to a degree would be a waste of valuable time and, in 1946, at the age of eighteen, he entered the Seminary of the Scarboro Foreign Mission Society. This, it should be explained, was not really a manifestation of any powerful urge to serve in the foreign mission field. On the contrary, it was a product of the feeling that there must be fewer recruits available for the missions than for service at home and that to undertake something difficult would be of more use than to do something that seemed to him easy. This boyish enthusiasm for self-sacrifice remained with him through a strenuous year in the novitiate. In the first year in the Seminary itself, it led him to impose an ill-considered restraint on the demands of a healthy appetite at the same time that he was driving himself, in study and exercise, beyond the limits of his adolescent strength. By the end of the year he was on the verge of physical and nervous collapse. At the request of his family the Seminary agreed to release him and he was persuaded that he should build up his health before deciding on his next step.

A summer spent mainly out of doors, with plenty of good food and rest, soon put things right. He was brought to realize that his difficulties at the Seminary were the direct consequence of his own mistakes and had been brought about by his own immaturity; it came as a shock but it taught him a valuable lesson. He never again allowed his ability to work to be impaired by neglect of his health. He had learned too, something of the virtue of patience and was willing to listen when he was urged to go back to university and complete his course for a degree.

The university he chose was St. Francis Xavier, in Antigonish, Nova Scotia. It was a fortunate choice. There he found teachers who, if their heads were perhaps in the clouds, had their feet firmly planted on the ground. His interest in social problems, which had been sparked by the stories brought back from Europe by the veterans he had known at Loyola in the period immediately after the war, found guidance and direction at St. Francis Xavier. He became intensely interested in the co-operative movement which had been developed among farmers and fishermen in Nova Scotia, largely through the instigation and encouragement of some of the priests from Antigonish. It was there too that he made the happy discovery that the need for priests was no less urgent in his beloved native Newfoundland than it was in more distant places. Gladly he offered his services to the Archbishop of St. John's and was readily accepted. In 1950 he received the degree of B.A. (summa cum laude) from St. Francis Xavier. He had completed his studies in philosophy there, so that when he entered the Theological College of the Catholic University of America in Washington, D.C., he required only four years to complete his preparation for the priesthood.

Vacations also contributed to his education in many ways. Immediately following graduation from St. Francis Xavier, he spent some weeks in Combermere, Ontario, acquainting himself with the views on social service of the Baroness de Hueck (Catherine Doherty). Then he joined his family, who had driven out to Vancouver. While he was in British Columbia he met the late Most Reverend J. J. Charbonneau, former Archbishop of Montreal, and had the good fortune to make a trip to Alaska and back in the company of that remarkable man. On the drive back east, he found opportunity to visit the "Friendship House" which the Baroness had founded in the Negro district of Chicago. Before going to Washington and the Seminary, he had time enough in New York for a visit to Friendship House there and for a few days' voluntary service in the settlement house of the Catholic Worker organized by Dorothy Day; thereby acquainting himself with some of the problems of social workers in a great city. Characteristically, he emerged from this experience wearing a cast-off pair of shoes, having given his own good ones to some unfortunate derelict. He could never be trusted to keep new shoes or gloves or overcoats.

His last vacation from the Seminary, in 1953, was spent in Europe. He visited Paris and some other parts of France; Italy, including Rome; and had a brief glimpse of London. But everywhere he went, his interest was in people and ideas rather than in places. One of the high spots of his tour was his visit to Eau-Vive, the discussion centre established near Paris by Jean Vanier, whom he had known at Loyola. And he spent two of his precious weeks on a hiking tour in Germany with a Catholic Youth Group, which included young people from Egypt, Spain, the Netherlands, England, France and Germany, all of whom were attracted by the opportunity to combine a pleasant outdoor holiday with earnest and wide-ranging discussions of the problems of youth in the modern world.

There was one more year in Washington and then, in May 1954, he was ordained in St. John's by Archbishop Skinner and was assigned to St. Patrick's Parish.

What sort of man was this newly ordained young priest? A loving friend, who knew him all his life, wrote this:

"At the risk of seeming uncritically admiring I might as well say that he was the best human being I have ever known. Really good people are fortunately scarce, for the rest of us would be shown up too often and too much, but there was nothing in Charlie that displayed even the smallest taint of conscious virtue or criticism of anyone else. He simply saw things differently and marched to Thoreau's different drummer.

I have never met anyone who was so completely free from what somebody called 'the contagion of the world's slow stain'. He had a curious innocence that was the very opposite of ignorance, of the seamy things of life, as if he were walking hip-deep through mud, was fully conscious of it but paid no special attention to it and emerged from it without a scrap of it sticking to him. He had also an extraordinary capacity for taking people in the mass as they were . . . He liked people and that was that, and was willing to work his guts out for them without for a moment considering whether they were worth it or not."

St. Patrick's is a very large parish and included at that time an area which had become known as "The Brow", on the upper slope of the hills on the south side of St. John's harbour. It had come into being as a sort of shanty-town during the depression years before the war and, being outside the limits of St. John's, lacked many of the amenities of the city. Father Charlie, as the youngest and most physically fit of the priests at St. Patrick's, soon found himself regularly assigned to the steep climb up the South Side hill. It was not long before all the inhabitants were his friends. Apart from his more strictly pastoral duties, he was organizing entertainments and discussion groups for them or advising on the preparation of a petition to the City Council for recognition of their needs. At that time the summit of his ambition was to see a church built on the Brow and to be installed as its first pastor.

Presently, however, he was transferred to the Cathedral Parish and, while he never lost his interest in his friends on the Brow, he could no longer take any active part in their affairs. Among his new duties was that of calling on the sick in the hospitals within the parish. He discovered there, from time to time, sailors from the Portuguese fishing fleet. For four hundred years, Portuguese fishermen have come out annually to fish on the Grand Banks. St. John's offers the nearest harbour where they can take refuge from a bad storm and the nearest hospital for any sailor who suffers a serious accident or becomes dangerously ill. There is a long tradition of friendship but nevertheless few Newfoundlanders speak Portuguese and many of the fishermen know no English. Father Charlie had a natural flair for languages. The French he had acquired at Loyola had become quite fluent during his summer in Europe. Now he undertook to learn Portuguese and his progress was rapid. In the summer of 1955, the Portuguese Government presented to the Cathedral a statue of Our Lady of Fatima, which was carried in procession through the streets of St. John's, escorted by four thousand Portuguese fishermen. It was Father Conroy who translated the Archbishop's speech of acceptance and repeated it in Portuguese for the benefit of the visitors. It was characteristic of him, too, that when, some years later, he found himself briefly in Lisbon, he made a quick trip to the coastal region where the Grand Banks fishermen had their homes and visited a number of families there, to their great delight.

Another duty which came his way was the editing of the diocesan monthly, the "Monitor". This gave him an opportunity to cultivate a talent for journalistic writing and also photography. He had always been an enthusiastic photographer; now he began to think of his camera as a source of illustrations for the paper, and to aim his shots accordingly. All this was to prove useful experience later.

Happy as he was to be among his own people in Newfoundland, he could never ignore a call from anyone in need of help. So, when Archbishop Skinner asked him if he would be willing to go to Latin America, he scarcely hesitated. Before his departure, he was granted a long holiday. His sister had entered the Sacred Heart Order and was taking her final vows in Rome in July 1960. He flew over to Europe in June and, after attending a Conference of Catholic journalists in Lisbon, he joined his mother and stepfather in Vienna and travelled with them through Northern Italy and then to Naples and Rome. Everywhere he found old friends or made new ones. Across a hotel dining room in Bologna he recognized an American he had met in Germany on his previous European trip, seven years before, and had not seen since. There was a joyous re-union. Entering a small cafe in Vienna, he saw another priest seated by himself and decided to speak to him. Coming back after five minutes of lively conversation, he was asked if his new acquaintance spoke English. He said, "No." "French then?" "No". "Well, you don't know any German. What language were you speaking?" "Oh, we spoke Latin".

After the ceremony in Rome, his sister sailed with her mother and stepfather for Halifax, while he flew to the Holy Land for a brief visit there, before returning by air to Newfoundland. A few weeks later he was on his way, via Montreal, to New York to meet his new colleague, Father Richard Morse, from the London diocese, and to fly with him to South America. For what happened thereafter, up to that fatal day in 1966, let him speak for himself.

Only when the plane left the St. Lawrence river behind and headed south to New York did it seem that this voyage to South America was really under way. But there was not much time for thinking about it. Father Richard Morse, my companion in arms, reached New York from Toronto five minutes before I got in from Montreal, but it took thirty-five minutes of running around — to Pan-American and back to Panagra — before we met. Idlewild is a city of air terminals and I nearly got lost in it as, in fact, my valise did, although it turned up a day later in Lima.

In a little over an hour we were off again, this time together and in a jet plane. We flew over Cuba where lights were twinkling at 2 a.m. and landed at Tocumena airport, Panama. It was raining there, as it had been in New York, but with a difference. There were pleasant, rich, growing smells. It was like going into a greenhouse. We took off again after half an hour, flying at 575 m.p.h. at 35,000 feet, with an out-door temperature of forty-five degrees below zero. That's how we crossed the Equator, far beyond Neptune's reach.

Just past Quito in Ecuador, and within a few miles of the Equator, we flew over the snow-capped peak of a mighty volcano, and at 9 a.m. on Sunday morning we reached Lima where we came in for a landing over the waves to be greeted by a familiar smell from a nearby fish-meal plant. It was like caplin on the gardens in Spring in Newfoundland. We are to spend a couple of days here before getting a plane to La Paz, Bolivia. From there we are to go on to Cochabamba where we are to train for our work in Latin America, Father Morse representing the Diocese of London, Ontario, and I, his partner, the Archdiocese of St. John's, Newfoundland.

Spring is well advanced in Lima and already roses are beginning to bloom. People at home set their watches ahead or back when they travel across Canada, but it is difficult to accept the idea that one can leave the watch alone and push the calendar ahead or back six months.

1

Income taxes are low here, but import duties are high, especially on cars. In a way one can be grateful for this, for the traffic is murderous enough now. Nobody can keep a car going longer than a Peruviano and it is marvellous to watch these zombie cars of international makes converging at squares and circles with one rule in mind, as a friend said, "Whoever has the most nerve wins." Our taxi would have taken at least second prize if they had a competition. I'm sure I saw a tuft of grass growing on the quivering bonnet. The ceiling was upholstered with a blanket which had to be held up by the right fore-finger of the passenger in the front seat and by the corresponding digit of the driver who seemed accustomed to steering with his left hand only. Holy cards of the Sacred Heart and of Our Lady were prominent above the windshield. We passed one establishment advertising 'bombas', but found later that it referred to pumps.

We had been welcomed at the airport by Brendan and Edna Halloran, both of Newfoundland. They had made arrangements for us to stay with the Maryknoll Fathers with whom we are to be in training in Cochabamba. The Rest House is a gathering place for all South American Maryknollers and is a perfect place for learning about conditions down here. After Mass, breakfast and a couple of hours' rest we went with the Hallorans to visit the place where St. Rose of Lima lived in the golden age of this city.

One saint leads to another. It is a fact that Lima once had five saints at the same time. Well — three saints and two 'beati'. St. Toribio was once a bishop here; St. Francis Solano was a Franciscan superior who used the violin in winning souls. Living here at the same time were Blessed Juan de Masias, only recently beatified, and Blessed Martin de Porres. St. Rose of Lima, like St. Catherine of Genoa, lived as a Dominican tertiary. She remained in her own home in which many things are today as they were then. In the enclosed garden of her home palm trees reach up almost a hundred feet. The hermitage she built with her brother's help is still there, but everything is encased in glass for protection. Among other relics are a letter she wrote thank-

2

ing a friend for a gift of chocolate, some statues, pictures and a couple of books.

Blessed Martin de Porres, not yet fully canonized, has no special shrine, although every church in Lima seems to have a statue of him. His name has been given to the district on the far river bank where close to a hundred thousand people have settled in the last five to ten years, most of them in desperate poverty. "Fray Martin", Brother Martin, is the patron of these people. The nine priests, Columban Fathers from Ireland, who serve in the three parishes there, have the honour of having taken on the hardest assignment in the city of Lima. It is an undertaking for which they deserve to have a special claim on Blessed Martin.

A new bridge spans the almost dry bed of the Rimac, a beautiful modern bridge which trembles under one when trucks pass over it. Across the bridge a sign advertises 'IN-CA-COLA' and to the right is a mountain, San Cristobal, which has a huge cross on its top. Underneath, in scrawled, huge letters, drawn on the rock, is APRA, signifying Haya de la Torre's leftist political party.

We went on foot down a side street towards San Pedro Church and ran into a *procesion apotheosico* in honour of St. Judo Mateo, Apostle. It was most interesting. The figure of the apostle is wonderfully well executed, very old, mounted in silver. The whole thing is so heavy that it takes eighteen men to carry it and that not for long. An army band followed the statue, playing a strange, slow march. The rhythm was striking. The apostle swayed slowly from side to side, giving an impression of majesty. Every forty feet or so it would be set down and presented with flowers by leaders of various *confradias*. Six policemen walked on either side of the statue with sub-machine guns. It looked a bit incongruous, but people prayed and sang with good intent, if distractedly.

We leave for Bolivia tomorrow morning and will wait in La Paz until the Archbishop comes on Saturday. The language school is in Cochabamba, about forty miles from there. It must be reached by plane or train as there is no road.

3

It is a week now since we arrived here, and what a week! By now I must have twice as many red corpuscles in me as before. It is the body's main way of adapting to less oxygen content in the air. At first I moved and thought only half as well as normally, but now I could take on all of Bolivia with all its problems. Maybe it is what Captain Cousteau, who invented the aqualung, described as 'ivresse des profondeurs', only this is the heights.

The three days spent in Lima, waiting for a plane to La Paz, were more than interesting, and our education had an easy beginning there in the warmth of friendly hospitality. Maryknoll priests from all parts of Peru and Bolivia gave us the results of their many years of experience. Diocesan priests from St. Louis, Mo., and Boston, Mass., told us of their parishes in the Bolivian lowlands and on the more than twelve-thousand-foot high *altiplano*. Irish secular priests of the Society of St. Columban showed us around their three 'squatter' parishes on the other side of the city dump and the dry Rimac river-bed. By the time we boarded the plane for La Paz we felt we already had a good introduction to the problems of Latin America.

The plane traced down the sandy coast of Peru as far as Arequipa and then swung in towards the Andes around the nineteen-thousand-foot active volcano, *Misti*, to Lake Titicaca to land at La Paz, the city named for the peace it has never known. It opens out in a deep bowl filled with glistening tin roofs and Spanish colonial architecture. It is a city rimmed by mountains, some of them snow-topped but often hidden in cloud. About four hundred thousand people are housed there below the high plain on which the airport stands. The first time one sees La Paz, coming in from the bare, brown *altiplano,* one has to rub one's eyes.

We stopped for a breath at Cristo Rey parish, as anyone who lives at an altitude of around thirteen thousand feet needs either extra gills or a more generous supply of red corpuscles in the bloodstream — and the latter, Nature's choice, takes a few days to develop.

4

Two priests from the St. Louis diocese, Father Andrew Kennedy and Father Joseph Ryan, administer this parish of twenty thousand Catholics. They took us down to the lowest level of the town, to the hospitality of the Resurrectionist Fathers in Calocoto, a suburb of La Paz which is two thousand feet below the level of the airport. Here we found breathing easier and the air warmer. It was strange to find such a difference in one city.

The Resurrectionist priests had just moved into a new house, but they gave us a marvellous welcome. Their parish of San Miguel also counts twenty thousand parishioners, many of them Indians who speak only Aymara, the language of the Tiahuanacan Empire which preceded the Inca. Besides the care of the parish they have two schools where — believe it or not — they teach full-time.

The Papal Nuncio is not here now, but at the Nunciature his secretary, Fra Giuseppe Ferraioli from Rome, has given us a regal softening-up treatment. We have picnicked on the shores of Lake Titicaca, dined at the Nunciature, visited the parish of the Oblates (two Canadian, two French), the Jesuit College which was formerly a colonial mansion and has a lovely chapel, the huge cathedral, the folklore museum. We have seen two movies, one of which portrayed the life of Franz Schubert in Italian, with Spanish sub-titles and marvellous photography and music. During all this time we covered very many subjects, speaking mostly Spanish (or French, when words failed). So we are well on our way. Father Morse preached three times on Sunday to help out, and we have both taught catechism a few times with what seemed to be success at a neighbourhood clinic for mental patients.

I have taken two rolls of film (coloured). One picture I would love to have had but failed to get — a woman in a bowler hat driving sheep along the sidewalk and, thirty yards ahead, her two-and-a-half-year-old, bare-foot, behatted daughter, solemnly driving two little pigs along with a stick.

I have just finished reading 'Cabbages and Kings' and feel quite certain that O. Henry, besides knowing universal human nature, knew Latin America as well.

5

A few days ago we went out on the *altiplano* as far as Huatajata on the shores of the largest, brightest mountain lake in the world, Titicaca. Another day we visited the ruins of Tiahuanaco, a centre of civilization at least fifteen hundred years ago. And we have met the hard-worked priests of the city parishes, the Oblates in *Parroquia del Espiritu Santo,* the four Maryknoll priests who direct the parish of San Pedro, with a four hundred year old church and forty thousand parishioners. There are many others in similar situations.

Archbishop Skinner and Monsignor O'Keefe arrived today after attending the Marian Congress in Buenos Aires. They were met at the airport by two of the bishops of Bolivia (the Nuncio and the Archbishop of La Paz being in Rome) as well as by Father Morse and myself and several other priests. In spite of the fact that the government has announced a state of emergency because of political trouble in the Cochabamba Valley, their visit here should be interesting and enjoyable. Bolivia has many growing pains and, as in many other Latin American countries, emergencies — even revolutions — are normal. The population of this country, which is mainly pure Indian, retains a childlike affection for priests and religious, and the present government has shown much good will in leaving the Church free to do her work. Father Morse and I look forward to several good months of study and practice in mission work here in this country in the clouds — the 'beggar sitting on a golden throne'. We do not yet know what the choice of our apostolate is to be.

LA PAZ, BOLIVIA, NOVEMBER 21ST, 1960

Today my Spanish was learned on a golf course, the highest one in the world. The score was 110 — not bad, considering that the fairway was soggy, the greens hard, and I could never get the approach shots right. Yes, it was eighteen holes! Father Morse has a handicap of only three, but played too seriously to enjoy the game as I did. There were

6

no other living beings on the course besides ourselves and a guide-caddy — except several hundred sheep, a few pigs, an eagle, several birds that were strange to me, a bull and a half-dozen Indians.

The Archbishop and Monsignor O'Keefe were here for several days. We had waited here for them, postponing going on to Cochabamba which is much farther from La Paz than I had thought. Some years ago the Indians of Bolivia were armed by rival political factions. Once they had been given arms it was hard to get these arms back. Last week a massacre which took place in the Cochabamba Valley made the Archbishop loth to send us on there. Most people here agree that the trouble is over with the blood-letting, so when the Papal Nuncio's secretary confirms this, we'll be on our way — probably next Friday.

So far we have been enjoying a sort of educational holiday, a most interesting one. The next few months will give us more of the same, but when our school time is over I expect there will be lots of work to make up for the easy days. I keep saying that to soothe my conscience. We are having such an enjoyable time now that I wish I could send some of it along in the envelope.

COCHABAMBA, BOLIVIA. NOVEMBER 26TH.

Behold! We have arrived for our training, but already feel well-educated. We went out from La Paz yesterday on the *altiplano* to Viacha, thirty kilometres away. The parish there is cared for by 'Rhiney' Scherhof and Dave Raterman from St. Louis, Mo., diocesan priests like ourselves and similarly on loan. Dave was in his last year at the Theological College in Washington when I was in my first, so for us it was a reunion. The third priest in the parish, Father Dan Stretch, has just been appointed. He had taken us out in a jeep, first to a Fiesta Mass in a *campo*, then to a parish they would like to have us take over, and then across the fields to Viacha. For Dan a Christmas present is in prospect from

7

Dave and Rhiney — five thousand Indian parishioners from each.

The church in Viacha has walls of stone ten feet thick, a silver altar and several hundred years of history. The priests' house had just been turned over to a community of nuns from Colombia who had recently arrived and whose commitment is to visit various of the eighty missions of the parish, preparing the people for a mission. Last week Father Raterman heard confessions for sixteen hours straight — most of them first confessions. He says none of their group of eight priests is anxious to go home when they can get a response like that.

The Fiesta we attended began in an ancient church that had no illumination except from the open door, a broken circular window above it, and candles lit on the altar. It was filled with people, including babies tucked in blankets on their mothers' backs. Father Stretch asked them not to leave the church until after Mass, even if the dancers arrived before that, and for the band not to strike a note until then.

Father Morse and I sang 'Missa IX' Gregorian, secundum quid. I suppose it was the first time there was a Missa Cantata in the church. After Mass confetti was sprinkled on people and a statue of Our Lady was carried to the four corners of the village square, the band trumpeting away between times while the 'Hail Mary' was being said in Aymara, one of the two most common Andean Indian languages. Unhappily, but inevitably, these fiestas turn into drunken sprees, but the priest has some say.

We are in a lower altitude in Cochabamba, a city with palm trees, the second largest in Bolivia, with a population of two hundred thousand. In the Maryknoll School here there are about a dozen priests midway through their course in Spanish. They come from the Maryknoll Society, the St. James Society, (organized by Cardinal Cushing and only prevented from being known as the Boston Boys by the number of Texans and Mid-Westerners among them) and from the St. Louis, Mo., diocese. We have received a warm welcome from them. The school is on the outskirts of Cochabamba and is a pleasant and interesting place. It was once the residence of the German Ambassador.

COCHABAMBA, BOLIVIA. DECEMBER 3RD, 1960.

The letter from home arrived three days ago, in spite of the fact that communications between here and La Paz have been interrupted by rail and air strikes. It must have come by Indian runner.

Father Morse and I reached here by the last plane of the national airline that usually sends three a day down here. It looks as though the unions are putting a financial squeeze on the government to secure the dismissal of some political appointees — but it might be for bigger gains. The language school is in a backwater suburb of Cochabamba where political changes are not likely to be felt, but if we ever need to make a strategic retreat the cash is on hand to do it with. The Maryknollers in Lima and the Resurrectionists in La Paz would not accept any recompense for the hospitality they dispensed.

This Saturday afternoon is free. I have just come in from a splash in our tiled swimming pool under the hundred-foot-high eucalyptus trees. The sun is strong but the air is like a perfect summer day in Newfoundland. There was a little thunder from the cumulus clouds poised on the mountains that slope up from our back yard several thousand feet, but as the mid-summer rainy season has not yet begun, we'll get no more than an April shower (in December). Tonight a little party is being thrown to celebrate the feast of St. Francis Xavier, the arrival of Father Masciarelli, Superior of the St. James Society group — and the less recent arrival of two distinguished Canadians.

Father Morse is a month younger than I and was ordained a month later. He's a perfectionist, but in a less busybody way than I might tend to be, that is, a self-perfectionist rather than a reformer of others. We have many points in common, bad memories for practical things, for example. He has a greater flair for languages but was hardly ever

9

outside the Province of Ontario and is self-conscious about the limitations such a calamity entails.

The Archbishop did not come down here. He must be back in Newfoundland by now and we hope soon to get word of his impressions and decisions. He made a very good impression on everyone who met him. He must be dizzy from the urgent appeals made to him and with the accumulation of information.

The day before yesterday I visited an old Franciscan monastery where I met a Bolivian priest, a Father Leus, who has published several books in Aymara and has others ready to be printed. He writes in Quechua too, the Inca language, the most common of the South American tongues. He has a marvellous collection of Indian animal stories, with date and place and the name of the person who told him the story duly documented. A local disciple of Audubon made lovely illustrations for them. Other notebooks of his contain Indian songs, with a Spanish translation on the opposite page, really good lyric poetry, often paid for with a glass of *chicha*, the local corn brew. Here I stop.

COCHABAMBA, DECEMBER 11TH

Cochabamba and I accept the apologies of our friends for thinking of us as a village and peasants. Actually, the Cochabamba Valley stretches for many miles and comprises *quartels* and villages that saw little change between the Inca conquest and the land reform of about eight years ago. The present government came to power at that time by distributing arms throughout the countryside and weakening the army. A real reversal of power was thus created, but also a Frankenstein monster that is no longer a dutiful servant.

I had thought that the farther away from Petty Harbour in Newfoundland, the fewer would be the dogs; but Cochabamba, with a hundred thousand people, has just as many dogs per man as Petty Harbour. We have only six dogs in this house. Three of them are fat white balls that can only yip as yet, but one of the others is the best bass in the neighbourhood. Every night barking competitions are held between all these fearless property-protectors for miles around.

However, it is hardly fair to introduce this city of our language study by its dogs. I am reminded of Father Pat McCormick of Conche who had known Father Morse in his seminary days and who, in describing him to me, began by telling me he was a good ping-pong player. He went on then to mention that he had greater qualities than skill at indoor sports.

No, Cochabamba is the pearl of Bolivia. The climate is good all year round and at the present time summer is in full swing. The strawberry season is just over and roses are in full bloom. I was interested last week, when I went to the convent of the Maryknoll Sisters to offer Mass, to note that their breakfast reading entertainment was Dickens' 'Christmas Carol'. That was just to help them realise that white Christmasses are just as real as our Bolivian kind. The other night four of the Sisters rode up here in the back of a big dump truck with about thirty children, all with candles and lanterns in hand, to sing us Christmas carols. The dozen of us who are studying Spanish here serenaded the children back, but in English. The only carol we could all sing together was *Adeste, Fideles*.

Our classes here are along tutorial lines. Father Morse and I have a twenty-one year old law student from the university, Jorge Agreda, instructing us. He is president of the Catholic Action movement in the university and also of the *Frente Universitaria Catolica*, a political action group.

In the fifty years of its existence here, the university has been dominated by an anti-clerical spirit. That is, up to last year, when the Catholic group organized well and swept the university elections. These elections are important because the university is administered independently of the government, in departmental matters by faculty councils made up of professors from each faculty, together with representatives from unions in the area. Once a year the university holds a Fiesta to celebrate its independence, with

11

floats and verses savagely satirical of all local celebrities. This was the first year that the militantly Catholic students had their innings. Their poem-commentaries were read by a curly-haired child, dressed as an angel and carrying a huge club, in the Don Camillo tradition.

At the start of the university political campaign the local Communist Party on the campus helped the new Catholic group with paper for propaganda, etc., hoping to split the conservative vote. When they realised that the tide was turning more swiftly than they had planned and was getting beyond their control, there were incidents of violence that culminated in a riot which the police had to stop with tear gas. The Catholics carried every post in the elections. This was quite a victory considering that it was accomplished mainly by the spontaneous efforts of three determined students who had no other funds than their own vacation earnings. The victory is more astonishing in the light of the fact that a pronouncement of this University Council carries such weight that the government usually acts on its published opinions. All Latin American universities have great political influence, but particularly that of Cochabamba because of its independence and its representation of all significant groups in this second-largest city of Bolivia.

LIMA, FEBRUARY, 1961

We are back in Lima, Peru, having finished an accelerated course in Spanish. The chosen parish is Monsefú, about five hundred miles up the coast. We are to be in Lima for a little while, arranging for carnets of indefinite residence in the country and attending to other formalities.

Today we visited the Canadian Embassy where we filled out registration cards and met the Ambassador, Alfred John Pick. He was pleased to see us because of the Monsefú Parish Incident which had attracted the attention of all Peru. He had followed it very closely, particularly after the

12

Upper: Fr. Conroy welcomed by local dignitaries as he arrived in Monsefú.
Lower: Fr. Conroy's body leaving Monsefú a few years later carried by his Peruvian friends.

Upper: Turgid water of irrigation canal used for washing, bathing in and drinking. Note carcass of dog recently dead of rabies floating in water. Lower: Some of the children in the school Fr. Conroy organized.

papers reported that the people there were hollering for Canadian priests.

The Monsefú Incident had been building up for years. Four years ago the people ran a priest out of town, reputedly because he was too fond of money, and they haven't had a resident pastor since. For some time they were looked after by diocesan priests from the Episcopal See city of Chiclayo, ten miles away. Then the people, represented by various brotherhoods and societies, combined to demand Canadian priests from a religious Order, preferably Franciscans. Eventually they became so pernickety about it that they locked up the Church and gave the keys to the local Mayor, instructing him to hold them and to refuse to give them up to the Bishop of Chiclayo until their demands were met. When it became apparent that appeals were being made to the authority of the state, the Bishop excommunicated the mayor and the officers of the various societies and placed the town itself under an interdict. Nothing like this had ever happened before in living memory, and it illustrates a crisis point in developments in the new Peru. Not that the Monsefuanos are very modern in their outlook — on the contrary, they are fanatically religious in a very traditional way. Nevertheless, the head of the 'Pro Indigena' committee anounced publicly that he considered excommunication out of date. They had asked for Canadians, having heard good reports of the Oblates, the Franciscans, the Quebec Foreign Mission Society and various orders of nuns who had come from Canada and were doing very good work. They wanted nothing more than a good pastor, he said. At this point I have to admit that if every parish in Peru with legitimate grievances made similar demands there would be great chaos. I am thinking, as I write, of the psychological problems facing us. I asked the Ambassador today if he would give me a short course in diplomacy, but he said he guessed I'd have to play it by ear.

Earlier this week we went to the Seminario de San Toribio where the annual Bishops' Conference is being held. There we met Bishop Figueroa of Chiclayo who wanted to talk to us about our new parish. He is a sick man but has the kind eyes of a saint. He is the soul of kindness and simplicity and is regarded with affection and reverence throughout Peru. He has had more than the usual share of worries of a person burdened with great responsibilities and has had also to contend with chronic ill-health. It will be a great privilege for us to give him what help we can.

He told us the situation would be difficult for us for only a short time, and thinks that if we accept the people as they are and make changes only slowly, he is sure we can do very good work. The excessive devotion of the people to images, he believes, is due to a lack of formation in the faith, but it will find its place later in a more balanced spiritual life, nourished by the sacraments. He said the leaders of the various parish and town organizations who had set the conditions for a solution of the difficulties and had refused to return the keys of the Church, were still under the ban of excommunication; but the keys had been returned indirectly and had been accepted without comment. The persons involved will be absolved from censure before our arrival, so that we can make a fresh start. I had looked up the newspaper acounts of the affair before calling on Bishop Figueroa, and it looks to me as though the insistence of the people on their Canadians may lead to a royal reception for us. Just the same, to please the fastidious flock in Monsefú, we may have to disguise our simplicity and give the impression we are members of an order. Dick Morse is all for the Order of Melchisedech, but I don't want anything more imposing than the Congregation of St. Peter, the Fisherman — *Sociedad de San Pedro, Pescador*.

This morning I celebrated Mass in the Fray Martin area which the Columban priests from Ireland have under their care. It consists of tiny shelters made of clay bricks or straw mats huddled together and holding many thousands of families who came down from the mountains in recent years, lured by the beauty and comparatively good wages of Lima. The Columbans have brought in reinforcements since we were here in November and have opened a new parish. This does not make them feel that they are moving ahead of the

14

need, however. About ten thousand of the people in the new parish were not there three months ago.

Our part of the country, on the northern coast, will be easier to know than this city of a million souls. Monsefú is about two miles from the coast and about ten from the diocesan centre, Chiclayo. We have only one mission, the fishing village of Santa Rosa on the sandy coast about three miles away. It never rains along the coast of Peru, but irrigation from rivers flowing down from the mountains can change desert into rich green fields and orchards. It is a curious fact that irrigation seems to produce more beautiful growth than rain which can sometimes be too abundant. Perhaps, too, it is the contrast between the oasis and the desert around it that makes the difference to one's thinking. The Humboldt Current, flowing from the Antarctic regions, gives the coastal area of Peru a good climate, even though we are only a few degrees below the equator. There is a sogginess in the air in Lima, with temperatures in the eighties. It will be hotter in Monsefú, but the heat will be dry and bearable and the prevailing westerly wind, coming in from the ocean, will always be cool.

The people of Monsefú are independent of the hacienda system which keeps many Peruvian workers on land that does not belong to them. Like many other coastal towns of Peru, the population is well mixed with Indian, Spanish, Negro and oriental elements.

LIMA, FEBRUARY 11TH, 1961

Two and a half weeks have gone by very quickly and, with one thing and another, there seems to be more to do now than when we arrived. Today, at last, we heard from the Archbishop and learn that I am to be pastor. A copy of the contract has been sent to the Papal Nuncio here and, as the Bishop of Chiclayo is also in town, I expect we'll be on the move very soon.

And now I'll have to stop saying bad things about pastors. One of the newly-ordained Maryknoll priests who was

15

studying with me in Cochabamba said he didn't think parish priests were so bad, but I pointed out to him that he had, as yet, no empirical knowledge to talk from.

We have had white cassocks made and, since they make straw hats in Monsefú, we may be able to find some shelter against the sun — maybe a gaucho hat. The people have made it clear that they don't want diocesan priests so, for a little while, until we get to know them and they us, we are to indicate that we are members of a religious society. We are then to be '*La Sociedad de San Juan de Terra Nova y de Londres*' and, as an ace in the sleeve, we have even had a rubber stamp made — in the best Peruvian tradition.

LIMA, FEBRUARY 12TH.

We are to be here in Lima only three more days. The Bishop of Chiclayo thought it best for us to wait until after Ash Wednesday to make our debut in Chiclayo — maybe to avoid the processions and the unnecessary chances of being shot up. Upon our arrival the leaders of all the organizations who were excommunicated last November will be released from censure and the Messianic Age will begin.

In Monsefú, the people will be assembled in the village square, with three brass bands playing all at once ancient *huainos, cuacas* and marches; the *banderas of the confradias* (flags of confraternities) will float in cool sea breezes under the equatorial sun; the two young *gringo* priests will be embraced and extolled in endless oratory by the mayor and *jéfes* of the town and they, in turn, will speak to all the gathering in warm and flowing Castillano — their white-cassocked figures framed against the sunset. Then Operation Cobweb will begin.

CHICLAYO. FEBRUARY 17TH, 1961

My eyes are closing, not, I think, from work-weariness, but from the change of climate. Chiclayo is about the same distance from the ocean as Lima is, but the air here is much

16

drier. We are at Hotel Turista, one of a chain run or subsidized by the government and one which would compare well with, say, the Three Falcons of Copenhagen. I do not exaggerate.

We arrived here yesterday afternoon in our new Toyota jeep which is just as solidly built as an English Land Rover and is more powerful. It came from Archbishop Skinner just for the asking. A week ago I got stuck in the middle of a river with it 'saving half an hour' in bringing one of the Boston priests to a hacienda for his week-end assignment. In spite of the fact that the water was up to the brake pedals nothing was damaged, and today I gave it a good, and this time successful tryout in deep mud between Monsefú and our fishing village parish mission, Santa Rosa.

We should have left Lima two days ago, early enough to get to Chiclayo by 7 p.m. but the Papal Nuncio, Archbishop Carboni, phoned us to ask if we had seen the Minister of Justice — or the President of the Republic. The first we had tried to do, but in vain; the second had never been mentioned by anyone nor, on our part, even thought of. So we postponed our 5 a.m. departure and went later in the day to the Nunciature to meet the Minister of Justice. He was to be there for a banquet in honour of Bishop Swanstrom of the U. S., who runs the biggest voluntary relief organization in the world, and other members of international relief agencies. Halfway through the banquet the Minister was called to the phone. He came back to say that the President of the Republic, Manuel Prado, sent his regards and salutations to everyone and would see the two Canadian priests at 10.30 the next morning. They all clapped us and, later, over a glass of Strega, the Nuncio said jokingly, "They are important people and they don't even know it."

The next morning the Minister of Justice called for us and took us to the President who thanked us in advance for settling a difficult problem for Peru. While waiting in the ante-room we met the head of the Air Force and several other V.I.Ps. We also met the Prime Minister, Pedro Beltran, who in this country is not as much of a big-shot as the

17

President. A delirious morning. It seems anything we need, we can use all the powers of government to get.

The problem of Monsefú seems to have settled itself. This morning we drove over there from Chiclayo and found people fixing up the mud-brick parish house. Bishop Figueroa had told us he thought the house would be habitable, but it hasn't been lived in for four years. Today we found busy people painting and getting together beds, furniture, cooking utensils. They are also preparing a bang-up party — and I mean just that — to celebrate the installation on Sunday. A half-Chinese owner of a confectionery store asked if I knew what *cohetes* (rockets) were. He said the ones that will be used in Monsefú will seem like atom bombs.

CHICLAYO, PERU, MARCH 2ND.

The Vicar General of the diocese, Monsignor Mondonedo, came with us to Monsefú on Sunday, February 19th in our Toyota Land Cruiser. It felt like a military expedition because the seminarians who came along to serve Mass half-expected to be met with a shower of rocks. The fierce anti-clerical movement of the last few years here has taken the form of being anti-diocesan rather than anti-religious-orders. As we are now the 'Sociedad de San Juan de Terranova y de Londres' we escape the odium poured forth on the *curas* of the diocese. ·

At the edge of town we had to abandon the jeep to become part of a procession which swallowed us up. Father Masciarelli, head of the St. James Society, who had come from Lima to launch us, seized my camera and took pictures of us being showered with rice and flowers. There were two brass bands and untold thousands of people. Every now and again a member of one of the committees would shout "*Viven los Padres Canadienses!*" while a huge Canadian flag was waved, or "*Viva Monsefú Catolico!*", to which everyone shouted back, "*Viva!*", while rockets roared.

We went around the Plaza Principal and up a ladder of a staircase to the Palacio Municipal to be treated to several eulogies and welcomes and given the keys of the church. Then on to the church for the oath of fidelity and the installation of the new parish priest — me.

The church is large and its central attraction is the statue of the *Senor Cautivo*, Our Lord as a prisoner, a life-size, realistic, carved wooden statue, clothed in purple velvet, with a golden crown of thorns and a silver chain binding the hands. For our day of inauguration the *Senor Cautivo* was taken from its side-altar shrine and placed above the main altar. Monsignor Mondonedo administered the oath and, in spite of age and infirmity, delivered a rousing sermon. While I was vesting for Mass Father Morse spoke and afterwards, in a few words, I told the people that we had to bury the past — I almost said 'the hatchet' — and concentrate on being one family.

We went from Mass to a champagne breakfast at the Centro Social, a library-and-homecrafts centre nearby. In the church the sweat ran like tears down our faces. The heat here is terrific but is only rarely unbearable. There is a great difference between sun and shade, and the cool, surprisingly dry breeze blowing in from the Humboldt current a few miles off shore, brings blessed relief.

The parish house is fit to live in, having been newly painted inside, so we went back to Chiclayo for our things which we had left in the care of the hotel, and moved in. The women of the Pro Defenso committee had put up new beds, supplied linen, a three-burner kerosene stove, and enough cooking utensils, tables, chairs, etc. to serve our needs. At the back of the house there is a bathroom with running water for shower, toilet and wash-basin. The water runs from a barrel on the roof of the annex which must be filled by hand.

The first week in our new parish began in tragedy when, on Monday, the day after the installation ceremony, a train-truck collision occured on the edge of town in which twelve men were killed. Ten of them were farm workers from this parish. It was the worst accident in the history of the town — "the inexorable reverse of the medal" as the local poet phrased it, after the celebrations of the day before.

We shared in the sorrow of the people and they were grateful to God that we were on hand and able to help. We had blood on our hands as we administered Extreme Unction.

Later in the week I visited the parish of Lambayeque with Father Fernandez, Chancellor of the diocese. There are two Spanish Dominicans there, one a round, jovial, wise and holy priest; the other a bantam curate who was teased by his pastor for loving co-operatives more than the Blessed Virgin. We went with them to see the parish's summer camp, run by Dominican nuns, at San José on the coast, and we swam in the surf and raced on the beach. The Toyota is great for getting through sand and coping with conditions that would stop most vehicles. We need it chiefly for getting to Santa Rosa where there are three thousand people — all fishermen.

MONSEFU, PERU, MARCH 14TH

The two-room house was made of mud bricks, without windows, and the doorway opening on the street gave very little light to the inner room. By candle-light I read the questions in Spanish from the Rite of Toledo in preparation for Holy Viaticum. The ninety-year-old woman answered, prompted by the family, "*Si, te creo,*" — Yes, I believe it — to each of nine points of doctrine. She had made her confession as best she could. I turned to open the pyx, and one of the sons-in-law chose that moment to announce that the old lady had never been married by the Church! The eighty-year-old groom was present. He was willing to make his confession and give his consent to the marriage. So Juliana Chafloque, at the age of ninety, with the last of her strength made her first confession, received Viaticum as her first Holy Communion, was confirmed, married and annointed, all in less than an hour. This is out of the ordinary, but it tells something about the pastoral problems of Peru.

Monsefú is possibly the most traditionally religious town in Peru. Besides the thirty-two statues in the church, many of them with side-altar shrines, there are many more scattered throughout the parish in private houses. These privately-owned statues are brought to the church yearly for Mass, often followed by a procession. The people come in droves to arrange for Mass to be offered on particular days, especially for their dead, with Monday as their first choice, the *Dia de Animas*. They want vigils and responses too, and have driven us back to the books to find points of liturgy that are more familiar to them than to us. A *vigilia* is the first nocturn of matins for the dead; a *responso* is either the *libera* over a catafalque or prayers for a funeral procession from the Rite of Toledo. If the *responso* is in the family home, there is on display a photograph of the deceased, with funeral ornaments and a line of women mourners on each side of the room, all holding candles and all crying at once. The men stay in the outer room. If the family can manage the expense, an orchestra is brought in too, fiddle, saxophone and clarinet, to render an authentic dirge that comes from the depths of time.

As our energies in the main are to be directed towards instruction in the faith and increasing the sacramental life of the people, Father Morse and I are trying to get out from under some of the weight of mourning. But for a while we must go along with customs, good and bad, because any brusque change will be disastrous.

There are about eighteen thousand people in Monsefú and its immediate environs, not counting the three thousand at Santa Rosa. In the national census which will be taken this year and in a parish one which we hope to take, we should get an accurate idea of the numbers in the parish and their 'sacramental standing' in the Church. With such a big family to look after we shall need to develop a lay apostolate and will be looking for help in all directions. A promise of two more priests before the end of the year makes for our greatest comfort of mind. If we can only arrange for the Sisters of Mercy to come next year it will be a tremendous help.

The biggest problem in bringing in lay apostles from outside will be financial. Here, for instance, a teacher in a primary school earns between six and eight dollars a month;

a person with a university degree, teaching in high school, might earn as much as forty-eight dollars a month. The cost of living, as Peruvians live, is low here, but anything imported is expensive.

I was distracted while writing, a minute ago, when an old lady called to present us with a chicken 'for our soup'. I don't know how to handle a live hen, so it is walking around the kitchen now, awaiting the arrival tomorrow of our cook who loves *animalitos* — little living things. She comes from a fishing village a few miles up the coast and speaks German as well as Spanish. She worked for many years with a German family in Europe and in the Caribbean until she decided to come home. I hope we can begin to forget about food problems now.

We had our first Fiesta with a procession the other day to celebrate the mid-year feast of *Senor Cautivo*, the 'Captive Lord', the most venerated of the images in this parish excessively devoted to images. I read my Office and a good part of the second book of Samuel from a pocket Bible in the two and a half hours the procession took to go through the streets of Monsefú. The statue was carried on an 'anda' by strong-shouldered *devotos,* most of them bare-footed. The band following behind, played slow marches, composed by the Incas or perhaps by their predecessors in the far past. We stopped often to duck under wires or to permit a *devoto* to pin his gift of money to the vestment of the statue, and five times for hymns and prayers. I frequently got a block ahead of the procession, lost in the story of David and Saul.

The people of our fishing village, Santa Rosa, have asked to have the *Senor Cautivo* statue for a ceremony of thanks-giving for the saving of their village from a tidal wave last November. The mayor has written me suggesting sending the *Cautivito* or small image instead, claiming that traditionally the large one never leaves Monsefú. His motivation is not too obscure. As all the arrangements had been made, including the printing of a programme, and as I must re-establish the principle of non-interference of the municipality in affairs of the Church, I refused to change the plans. I wrote him, explaining that the image is not the property of any particular society, but of the Church for which I have been given responsibility. I said that in furtherance of the spirit of unity in the parish, this is a good idea. And I invited him to come to Santa Rosa for the ceremony. I remembered afterwards that by tomorrow all images should be veiled. The season of Lent is so little recognized here that I made the promise without remembering. And now it is too late to back out.

Monsefú reaches back beyond history. It is said to be the primeval settlement of this valley — one of the many valleys that produced individual civilizations centuries before the Inca domination of the Andes and the subsequent systematic suppression of racial memory which the Inca Empire, in its plan of expansion, imposed on conquered peoples. The names of many of the people in this area, as well as that of Monsefú itself, do not belong to the Quechua or Inca language and there are traces of customs and manual arts that come from the remote past. Perhaps I should attempt to pluck from out of that past some of the early figures whose activities helped to shape the present.

It seems that long, long ago, this river valley of ours was invaded from the sea by a prince by the name of Naynlap who let it be known that he would never die. He established as the god of his people a precious stone, an emerald of great size, to which the people were to bring smaller ones in tribute. Eventually he either went quietly into exile or died in secret. At any rate, his descendants had to maintain the bluff of his immortality as best they could. Then came the Inca conquest of the coastal peoples and, within a century or so, the Spaniards arrived. Cieza de Leon, Spanish soldier-historian, writing in 1548, claimed that most of the people around here could not speak the language of the Incas, even though the latter were noted for their insistence on uniformity. He gives the Incas credit, just the same, for establishing one of the best systems of government he had ever heard of. His observation, based on his personal knowledge, brings to mind that St. Thomas More, when he wrote his 'Utopia' thirty years earlier for the private

23

amusement of his Amsterdam friend and host, Peter Giles, suggested that Christian nations are often less just than heathen ones.

The Spanish historian observed — and this still rings true — that the people of this northern coast are hospitable and polygamous, love to dance and 'never leave off having a bowl of chicha (corn beer) in the hand'. He thought the local language was the devil's tongue but, forty years later, when the Archbishop of Lima, Saint Toribio, came through on a pastoral visit, it was recorded of our neighbouring parish of Eten, 'The parish priest knew well the Yunga or fisher language which is what the Indians speak.' Later on, in 1644, the parish priest of Reque, another parish bordering on ours, published a book called 'The Art of the Yunga Language'. The word 'yunga' was picked up by the Spaniards from the Incas for whom it meant 'hot land'. The local name for the language was 'Mochica' from the race-name of the people of this area. It is now a lost language, having disappeared completely.

One of the many interesting documents of the early Spanish times on our part of the coast is a will made by one of the Indian nobles of the locality who, in one section, referred to his 'widows'. In the context this seems to refer to the wives he put aside when he became a Christian.

In the early part of the Spanish era the most important city in the north was Zana where St. Toribio died on the way back to Lima from a missionary journey. It is only thirty miles from Monsefú and in it there still can be seen the impressive remains of fourteen churches. It was destroyed by a flood during the Spanish era. There is a legend that this happened after a Corpus Christi procession that turned into a brawl. It seems there was a quarrel among the men who were to carry the canopy and in the scuffle someone was killed and the Blessed Sacrament fell to the ground.

In 1720 many of the people from Zana moved to Lambayeque which at that time was also much more important than it is now. Floods and other catastrophes seem to have been associated with the founding as well as the abandon-

24

ment of settlements in this area. Monsefú itself is thought to have been founded after a plague decimated the population of Callanca, a place six miles from here which is part of our parish. According to an article by Napoleon Gallina which appeared in a Chiclayo newspaper in 1945, our parish was founded in 1536. At first it was under the jurisdiction of Lima; then, in 1616, under the Archbishop of Trujillo. But the earliest parish records in our possession go back only to the baptisms of 1674. Chiclayo has grown in importance in relatively recent times and it was not until four years ago that the Diocese of Chiclayo came into being, with jurisdiction over Monsefú and all this area.

Epidemics have devastated our town many times since its founding. The records show that in 1839 there were two hundred and fifty burials in the space of three months; in that same year the church burned down; in 1847 small-pox took heavy toll; in 1868-69 seven hundred and twenty-one people died. Plagues have left bitter memories in Monsefú. At least three of them are commemorated by processions annually — two in which the Captive Lord statue is brought out and one, with the Blessed Sacrament, which is referred to in the programme as 'The Most Holy One of the Epidemic of the Black Vomit'. This year, the only outside procession with the Blessed Sacrament will take place on Corpus Christi.

Father Francisco Martinez, one of the parish priests of the past in this parish, must hold the world's record for length of service. He came here first as a curate in 1750 and died here seventy-six years later; and for most of that time he was in charge of the parish. In the old days, when there were only about three thousand people in the town, there were two and sometimes three priests here. Usually the parish priest was of the diocesan clergy and the assistant from a religious order. Judging from the baptismal records of those earlier days, most parents were properly married. There is no doubt that the close association between the government and the Church in the Spanish dominions was at least partly responsible for this good showing. Since moral offences could be punished by public whipping at the hands of the lay authority, it is not surprising that open sinning was regarded as an unprofitable venture. This tradition of improving morals by means of legal pressures and sanctions may well explain why we find in our people so little spontaneous participation in the things the Church holds most dear. As late as 1837 the Bishop, during a pastoral visit to Monsefú, left instructions with the parish priest to send him a report each year on 'the state of souls' in his parish, listing the families by name and requiring their status to be declared, whether slave or free. The legal inheritance from Ancient Rome reveals itself in the solemnity and the careful wording of these parish records of a bygone day.

A knowledge of what has shaped the past of our people helps us to a better understanding of them and of the problems that confront us in separating the living faith from the almost pagan practices which have become associated with it. If we could give it back to them in its beauty and simplicity, a lifetime of service would be a small price to pay for the privilege.

MONSEFU, MARCH 25TH, 1961.

I am writing this by candle-light tonight because, not very long ago, it began to rain, though ever so gently, and the Chiclayo power system was so astonished, *se apogo* — it pegged out.

Bad news. Father Dick Morse is in hospital with a severe attack of hepatitis. I was expecting something to happen, but not anything so serious, even though it was the fate of more than half of the first group of the St. James Society (Boston) priests, to come down here. Dick's resistance has been low for some time. He has been unable to eat and has been losing sleep because of the blaring of bands, the thunderous explosions of rockets and the fervent 3 a.m. arguments in the square on which our house fronts. He has suffered also from the nocturnal massed choir of mosquitoes, about twenty squadrons strong, which we have at last dis-

26

couraged by putting plastic mesh over the septic tank exhaust and netting around our beds.

He is receiving good care in the hospital in Chiclayo but I think, after he spends a few weeks of complete rest there, he will be on his way home to Canada for a long period of recuperation. The people will miss him very much because, in the short time he has been among them, he has visited many of their homes and grown to know them and, to some extent, their problems.

During Holy Week while Dick was in hospital, I was more than busy. On Palm Sunday I was out of sorts because the distribution at the altar rail was little short of riotous. A short procession was held outside the church in the morning, led by a cantor who sings from memory the melodies of his grandfather — not at all what the book says.

In the afternoon the popular procession took place, longer than the morning one, with a life-size image of Our Lord of the Branches riding on a real donkey. I walked behind the burro for the first part of the procession but was glad to be ushered forward after we had stopped and prayed at several stations on the way. I made a mental note of the fact that the priest was not so well vested as the donkey whose exquisite trappings were of velvet embroidered in gold. The work had been done locally and I could only marvel at the talent and artistry that lie hidden behind mud walls in our little community.

In these religious processions everyone is involved, down to the babies slung on the backs of their slightly bigger sisters, and up to the oldest patriarchs. The men keep to one sidewalk and the women to the opposite and while many of the people do not pray consciously, a religious spirit pervades throughout.

On Monday there was another procession, this time bearing the statue of the *Senor de Lunes Santo*, The Lord of Holy Monday. It is a very beautiful one of carved wood and like the rest of the old ones in the church, is painted realistically and vested in embroidered velvet. On the evening of Wednesday in Holy Week we were slated for the procession of *El Senor de los Siete Caidas*, The Lord of the Seven

27

Falls. This image has built-in springs which are timed to cause it to fall at appropriate intervals. In former times its hollow head was filled with animal blood so that when it collapsed a most dramatic effect was produced. Happily, this year, the band charged more than the majordomos were willing to pay, so they cancelled the procession of their own accord.

The band instruments used in these religious processions, in deference to the Holy Week liturgy, are usually flutes and a couple of muted trumpets, but the music is the same all year round — a slow, solemn dirge with a powerful beat.

The procession held on Good Friday night with another statue representing Christ in the tomb, *El Senor del Sepulcro,* took five hours to cover seven blocks. The hearse carrying the statue was illuminated by power from a gasolene generator on a tricycle cart. The bearers, twenty-four men, swayed from side to side in rhythm with the music and took a short step forward on every fourth beat. In times past this procession lasted all night, ending only at dawn. This year, mercifully, we reached the end of the way at midnight, having set out at 7 p.m.

Holy Thursday had brought unexpected consolation. There were about sixty-five confessions and communions — the average on Sunday being seven. The church was crowded and many kept vigil at the altar tomb. The old men chosen for the *mandatum* at the washing of the feet ceremony recognized it as an honour, but it was no mere formality — their feet were really dirty. Few of our parishioners wear shoes, nor is there any better reason than fashion why they should. The people were greatly impressed by this ceremony but, though I explained the motivation in flawless Spanish, I got the impression that I was not too well understood. The next day a woman asked me if I would come to her home to wash the feet of her mother who is unable to walk.

On Holy Thursday morning I went to Chiclayo for the Mass of Consecration of the Oils. Delegates from this and all the other parishes within easy reach of the diocesan centre had been asked for, both clergy and lay people. Meanwhile, in Monsefú, the customary representation of the Last Supper was placed in the sanctuary of the church — a table around which were placed the image of the Lord of the Branches, from Palm Sunday, and various other images from the church, representing the apostles. Bread and fruit were laid out on the table, and later some of it was brought to me.

The Easter vigil had been talked about in Lenten prayers and four busloads of people arrived from the fishing village of Santa Rosa. It was all very disorganized, but the solemn renewal of baptismal vows was gratifying.

It is a custom throughout Peru to call on famous preachers to give the "Three Hours' Agony" on Good Friday. There were no famous preachers available around here, but the Good Friday Brotherhood were obviously anxious to try me out and I decided to go along with the custom. Well, it *was* three hours, and it *was* agony. My mind was full when I started, but there were very few in the church. By the time the church was full my mind was completely empty. I used as the central theme the obedience of Christ on the cross.

News has just reached me that Father John Maddigan is coming down here to join me. This is as much a joy to me as it must be a pang for those he has been working with for the past few years. When I was a tender-foot in the Scouts he was second in command of our patrol and as great company then as ever since. I must write him to tell him what we need — a fly-swatter, a strong stomach and a gringo cook-book.

Monsefu, April 24th, 1961

Father Dick Morse has been called back to Canada by his bishop to recuperate from his recent illness. He left for Lima and home early this week and must, by now, be back in Ontario. The two weeks before his departure were not terribly busy, which was a good thing for me because I was more exhausted after the pressures of Holy Week than I had realised and was more than willing to lie low. On April

29

3rd, Dick spread the news from his hospital bed that it was my birthday. There were all sorts of salutations, including gifts of a pair of black nylon socks, a can of peaches, and a letter from home which arrived right on the button. I was invited to dinner at their convent in Pimentel by the Canonesses of St. Augustine who have helped us tremendously both here and in Santa Rosa. On my way there I went frolicking on the beach with a crowd of altar boys. While they chased one another I went swimming near a wrecked ship that is connected to the shore by hawser. Two waves that coincided in the surf knocked me flat and rolled me over, head over heels. I came up with a fat lip and a nozzleful of sand. I thought of Demosthenes and the gravel in his mouth and wondered if my preaching could be bettered by sinuses full of sand. It couldn't hurt the sermons anyway, I decided.

A few days after Dick's departure, Father Thomas Reilly of the St. James Society in Lima arrived for four weeks' rescue work. He had had little to do in that city for some months past, as his job as director of the Santiago Language School is not yet operative. He had visited us for a day, just after Easter, while Dick was still in hospital, and had sized up the situation and our great need. Then he suggested to Father Masciarelli, the Superior of the loosely-constructed band, that he should come here to help out for a month. And so it was agreed. It is a strange thought for me that a former pastor of about forty-eight years of age should be coming to me as temporary curate, bringing with him a mountain of canned goods and two dollars a day for his keep. Before coming he made sure that the Coldspot refrigerator we had purchased in Lima had been shipped to Monsefú.

Since Father Reilly's coming we have both had our hands full, especially over the past weekend. And Monday is a big day here, the day of souls — when the farmers around come into town to light candles in the church for their dead and to drink the local corn beer, chicha, with more devotion than on other days.

Father Reilly is holding the fort in Monsefú while I am enjoying a brief stay with the Wittwer family in this oil city two hundred miles north. I hope he won't be too exhausted after three days coping with the parish alone.

It was a confused getaway for me on Wednesday morning. Just as we were approaching the airport in Chiclayo I remembered that my ticket was still on the breakfast table in Monsefú. They don't sell tickets at the airport and it seemed quicker to go back to base than to try for a new ticket at the town office, so — hoping there were still enough minutes left, we jumped into the jeep, with Conroy at the wheel, and zoomed off. Just down the road, precisely when I was recalling that passage of 'Two Jinkers' which relates that "Our gardjen angels never knew of such an active season", the station wagon of the Canonesses of St. Augustine flagged us down. I very nearly didn't stop, but it turned out they had my ticket. I've had a series of guardian angels all my life, some temporary, some permanent.

I came to Talara on the promise of the International Petroleum Company to give us some used furniture from its stores that the Company doesn't need. A truckload and a half is already on its way to Monsefú. There are enough tables, desks and chairs among it to provide at least half the needs of our future community of priests and perhaps for the future convent as well. Although the furniture is pioneer and battered by time and termites, it can be fixed up. We have good carpenters in Monsefú.

I am enjoying my stay with Bob and Dolores Wittwer and, when free of the distractions of duty, the chance to communicate. I had met Dolores' mother on the train last February when I went to La Oroya in the high *sierra* to help out one of the St. James fathers. Her enthusiasm for helping missionaries must have been passed on to her daughter. When I board the train this afternoon for the return to Monsefú, I'll be laden with delicacies.

A few days before I came to Talara we held a meeting to organize distribution of relief foods that come from the

U. S. and are dispensed through the parishes. Monthly distribution is not difficult, but we are anxious to set up a refectory for young children — the four, five and six-year-olds — to give them a breakfast of hot milk and bread. It will cost thirty-eight soles a day, about $1.40, to have the bread baked, the powdered milk prepared, and all transported from Chiclayo. Thus, two hundred children will be fed at a cost of two 'reals' each. The kids will bring one real (less than half a cent) each. The rest we'll get by scrounging.

We have had word that Mother Imelda, the Mother General of the Mercy Order in Newfoundland, will be coming down soon to look over the lay of the land. The whole question of funds for building presbytery, convent and school is very complex and unsatisfactory, not only with regard to where they *can* be got, but also on the principle of where they *should* come from. The people of the parish ought to provide a good part of the necessities, but they are not accustomed to giving and they haven't known us long enough to have confidence in us. Luckily, the parish owns some property which we may be able to trade for more conveniently-located space and for building materials. But in all these questions of administration, construction, etc., — with all due respect to myself — I think they've sent a boy on a man's errand. I am reminded of the famous notice posted in a store window in St. John's, "WANTED: a boy to do a man's work." So, with me.

MONSEFU, MAY 10, 1961

Father Reilly goes back to Lima next week, but I think he may return. He has been a marvellous help, but I'll manage somehow on my own. After all, until our coming last February, there was hardly ever more than one priest here, except in the old days, long ago, when more priests were available. And I won't really be alone. The Mercy Sisters from St. John's will be here soon.

32

Laura, our cook-housekeeper, left us a couple of days ago to attend a wedding and is now thirty hours overdue. We were pleased when she came to us as she had had many years' experience in Germany with a German-Peruvian family and had later gone with them to Heligoland, Casablanca and, eventually, Haiti but, as we learned too late, not as cook. She has never learned to operate our Dutch stove which converts kerosene to gas and she is too old now, at sixty, to learn new tricks easily. Last night when I tried to turn cook myself to prepare a meal for Father Reilly's last evening here, I was appalled at the conditions I found in the kitchen where there was not one clean pot or utensil. Today, twenty-four hours later, I am still marvelling at the strength of Father Reilly's and my respective constitutions.

Good news! Mother Imelda and Sister Dorothy arrived in Lima a few days ago and were met at the airport by the Nuncio who carried their bags. They arrived here in Monsefú not long after our cook, Laura, returned. She explained that she had been ill and had not been able to get in touch with us. I gave her a month's salary and wished her well, but said I thought the work here was too hard for her. The matter of food and its preparation is of deep concern to us, especially in view of Dick Morse's experience. We cannot afford to take unnecessary health risks, but I could not explain to Laura that the head has reasons that the heart knows not.

We had arranged for the Mercy Sisters to stay with the Dominican nuns in Lambayeque, a few miles on the other side of Chiclayo; but when they walked into our kitchen and saw the chaos there they rolled up their sleeves, set to work and announced that they would move into this house for a while to set things in order and keep an eye on me. They were so keen on the idea that I put up very feeble resistance. However, it has not happened that way. The Dominicans in Lambayeque strongly advised them not to take up residence in the presbytery for fear of losing prestige in Monsefú. Mother Imelda and Sister Dorothy bowed

33

to the advice, but the former declared that if the Monsefuanos could really think she and Sister Dorothy were kept
women, they would also have to think that their parish
priest showed very poor taste. And so they are staying in
Lambayeque with the Dominican Sisters.

Every morning they come in by bus to Chiclayo for an
hour's language class. I pick them up afterwards and bring
them to Monsefú for the day. At the pace they are setting
for themselves they will know the town inside out within
a couple of weeks and will probably have found a new cook
for me in the bargain.

Mother Imelda, having taken a good look at my living
quarters, declared firmly that a new presbytery will have to
be built as well as a convent. Although I am a greenhorn in
matters of finance, and must rely very much on the experience of others, I feel that I must find a system for dealing
with our economic problems. The Maryknollers, who are
very well organized, depend to a surprising degree on home
contributions. A circle of about a hundred supporters is estimated to be able to take care of the needs of each missionary. They allow two dollars per day per man for food and
maintenance. We'll have to do something of the sort just
to keep this place from falling down around us, yet I know
I haven't the time to write a hundred people, even once a
year, seeking or acknowledging assistance. What little money we get from the people is eaten up in daily, minor repairs
to this house.

This is a well-to-do parish in comparison with others near
here, but money given goes largely to the various brotherhoods who sponsor fiesta occasions, and they put it into
brass bands and fireworks in honour of the saints. Money
given to the priest for parish needs is regarded as the price
of services rendered, something to be bargained about and
dickered over. There are reasons to be found in history for
this attitude, but I haven't yet found the way to deal with it.
Sooner or later, I am convinced, the people will have to
learn to support their own parish.

I often feel down-hearted these days, in spite of the fact
that there is always a supporting hand. And I wonder some-

times if the component elements of physical malaise and spiritual discouragement are not the same. Multiple frustrations and small problems, I find, produce a state of confused lethargy which is physical as well as mental.

In these moments of spiritual darkness I keep holding to the thought that God will not let this undertaking be a purely human one. The Nuncio in Lima kept saying to us, "By yourselves you can do nothing, but with the help of God you will work miracles." I am realising the truth of the first half of that sentence only too well. I can only cling to the hope that the second half will come to pass also.

LIMA, JUNE 14, 1961

It's an ill wind that blows nobody good. The thin air of the *altiplano* of Bolivia sends many missioners down to the coast on altitude leave once or twice a year to give their lungs a rest. One of these, Father Edward Feuerbacher, is now spending half his leave here in Monsefú, helping me. He is one of the priests from the St. Louis, Mo. diocese which has undertaken two parishes in Bolivia. He has sent me to Lima for a week's rest, a medical check-up, and a chance to see Reverend Mother Imelda and Sister Dorothy off on their homeward flight, while he takes care of my twenty-one thousand parishioners.

Shortly before Father Ed's arrival in Monsefú, Bishop Sanchez-Moreno, the new auxiliary bishop of the Chiclayo diocese, came out for an informal visit. He is a young man, only about a year older than myself. He was a lawyer before he became a priest and a member of the 'Opus Dei' institute. He has had no pastoral experience. The day of his visit was one of my busiest and, as I had no time to give him, I sent him to hear the children's confessions. I am growing arrogant!

It is hard to part with Reverend Mother Imelda and Sister Dorothy. I have treated them badly, letting them cook and clean house for me when they were not attending Spanish classes or getting to know our town, and I have not been of much help to them. I did attempt one day to help with the dishes, but I was called away to see about some work which was being done and was interrupted again and once again. When the dishes were done I was found asleep in a chair with the dish-towel, like a ribbon of merit, over my shoulder.

Somehow a knowledge of Spanish was not needed for the Mercy nuns to win the affection of the people. Mother Imelda wished she could tumble the little ones into a bath, but decided that would have to wait. Sister Dorothy turned them from chatterboxes into adoring angels in the church, with just a flick of the wrist. We had no trouble deciding on an ultimate site for school and convent. It will be 'Las Animas', a large, tree-bordered field owned by the parish and only five blocks from the church and the centre of town.

Bishop Sanchez-Moreno and all the well-to-do families in Chiclayo are anxious to persuade the Mercy nuns to start an English-speaking school there. The nuns say they will only consider doing this if they can start in Monsefú at the same time, helping us the more for having a Chiclayo house. No definite decision can be made as yet because Reverend Mother Imelda must first put the matter to her Council and, as her own second and necessarily last term of office will expire in August of this year, it may be her successor who will deal with the matter. She is a very wonderful person, as also is Sister Mary Dorothy whose puckish sense of humour makes her company a delight and somehow, without much knowledge of Spanish, makes it possible for her to communicate with the people. I have found myself that the most sensible people are often those gifted also with a sense of humour.

We had a *despedida* or going-away gathering at the Villa Maria Convent here tonight in honour of the Mercy nuns before their send-off. They are going back with an immense amount of knowledge of the possibilities as well as the problems of the parish which I could never have put into words. I am happy to think that it won't be long before they'll be back, in person or in envoy. As their plane took off I thought of the time, not so very long ago, when Reverend Mother Imelda came to Marystown in Newfoundland to visit the schools. I rowed her across the tide to the south side in our leaky dory, proud of my pulling ability. She had to show me how to tie up the dory that time, and this time she had to put my house in order.

Monsefu, June 27th 1961

The week in Lima gave me a valuable break from the cares and anxieties of Monsefú. A medical check-up proved that I am made of stronger stuff than my good friend, Father Tom Reilly who is now on a month's leave, recovering from early symptoms of hepatitis. On his return to duty he will take over the parish in the oil city of Talara, two hundred miles north of here, making him practically a neighbour of ours.

Father Ed Feuerbacher deserves all praise — every bit as much as Father Reilly. He was without electricity for most of the time I was away, but that was merely an inconvenience. His real discomfort was from amoebic dysentry. Yet he held the fort well. It was a queer sort of hospitality that kept him here at work and ill while I, his host, enjoyed time off. But he thought I needed the rest and I was easily persuaded to agree. While my back was turned he bought a desk lamp, a floor lamp and a record player for us, none of which we have been able to try out as yet, as the power has not been restored. I am writing tonight by the light of a lantern.

Today brought a letter from Archbishop Skinner advising me that Father John Maddigan will be in Lima by July 10th. Other happy news came from London, Ontario, telling me that two priests from that diocese are being sent down very soon to replace Dick Morse. The names, Cooney and Mooney, will make an impressive, if curious, addition to the Newfoundland side of the partnership. I am delighted to have all that help in prospect, but the mud-brick house here just will not accommodate four people without a radical transformation which it doesn't deserve. It needs replacement.

Nothing short of that would be worth the cost. For the next few months, at any rate, the London men will be at the language school, probably in Cochabamba, while the Vincentians in Chiclayo will be able to take care of Father Maddigan.

Things are looking up generally. The Wittwer family — Dolores and the two girls, rather — were here recently. They came, laden with gifts, a hundred huge oranges from a plantation near Talara, and groceries of all kinds. The girls are two little bookworms who were happier in the hotel in Chiclayo than in exploring as tourists. They returned home today, taking with them Dora Diez of Monsefú, for a week's training in health precautions and gringo cooking. When she comes back she will work at the presbytery as secretary for four hours a day and will double as cook for two hours.

Simon Lopez, who has been working here for the past month, has proved himself a treasure beyond price. He is looking after the church, sacristy and house and has even undertaken to wash the dishes.

The Archbishop's letter has made it clear that help will be given if the needs are made known. He writes, "I am afraid we may have given you the impression that you are so bound to a contract that you may not approach us on anything not foreseen in the contract," and goes on to say that an all-out effort will be made in October in the Latin American collection, inviting me to state our needs. So, I have decided to ask for a new rectory and for some arrangement which will make us independent, for the present at least, of local support. What local contributions we receive can then be channelled into repair of the church which is also sadly needed. Even at that, they won't be much. The average earning power of a man with a family here is no more than sixty cents a day.

Everyone who comes to Monsefú sees great possibilities for our work. Our people are intelligent and are within easy reach; and we have seen plenty of indication of willing co-operation on their part. Just the same, there are times when I experience a certain sadness of mind at my own incapacity for getting organized — even though this is something so inherent that I must learn to live with it. There are anxieties, too, about decisions involving putting trust in people without knowing them too well, and about whether certain age-old customs should be discouraged or approved; also about eventual building, ordered financing and responsibility for the others who are coming to join me. Most of all I am concerned about the socio-economic-religious backwardness of the whole area and the little it seems possible to do before a revolution takes the matter out of our hands.

It seems to me that in dealing with the people here I just have to find the tides of their own traditions, ride them carefully and guide situations slowly and with what wisdom I may acquire through experience and observation. As the ambassador told me, I must learn to play it by ear.

MONSEFU, JULY 9TH, 1961

Today I attended a soccer game. It was a good change from the confinement of the presbytery and the narrow streets of the town, to sit perched on a wall, looking down at an acrobatic game of football and a field full of people. I had just last night blessed the jackets of a new team, the Apostles, but unfortunately the blessing didn't do them any good.

On the way back to the presbytery I thought happily of John Maddigan who will be in Lima forty-eight hours from now. He will be delayed there, getting over the immigration hurdle and getting acquainted with that beautiful city, but will be in Monsefú in a matter of days. *Que bienvenido!*

I find myself in good spirits again after a period of malaise of mind and body which I find hard to explain. The human spirit is strangely affected by small things — hidden necessities which a change of environment exposes, the need for communication with friends, for instance, and for sharing worries that, for brooding on them, have become more demanding on the system than concentrated work. I wonder sometimes how long I would have lasted in the Russian labour camp that my friend, Monsignor Gerhard Fittkau

describes from his own experience in his book, "My Thirty-
third Year".

For the record I must recount what happened today to
a nylon windbreaker sent from home and valued at $5.00.

The customs officials added twenty per cent to the valua-
tion, labelled it 'Clothing of the genus of textiles of artificial
fibres', taxed it at a bit more than $5.00 plus twenty per
cent. Then they added a few more taxes, duly documented
as being under Laws 11424, 7695-11495, 12785, 12972, 12995
— this last was a $10.00 bite — 12972, and 13199 and, to top
it all off, a *poste aereo* charge of 12¢. The grand total came
to 439.76 soles, $18.00. Not feeling very patriotic, I said to
the Customs clerk, "Viva la Revolucion!" and told him to
return the package to the sender.

When I got back to the presbytery I packed a picnic
lunch and took off in the jeep, heading by a devious route
for Chongoyape where I was to meet the auxiliary bishop
on his return from pastoral visits in the mountains. I went
first to Lambayeque where I was invited by my friend,
Father Miguel, O.P., to have lunch with him and take a
siesta. This I did gladly. After lunch I was shown into a
spare room and supplied with a blanket which I very quickly found was already being used by an energetic regiment
of fleas. I am told that rats bring fleas, and I think these
creatures had been nesting in the unused room.

The Dominican priests in Lambayeque have built up a
model parish over a period of thirty years and they have
done a splendid job of restoring the church. Only now are
they beginning to renovate their own living quarters. We
hope to achieve physical restoration somewhat more quickly,
and, in fact, my reason for going to Lambayeque today was
to arrange for plans for a new facade for our chapel in Santa
Rosa, as the sea wind has weakened the front of the building.

After leaving Lambayeque I returned to Chiclayo where I learned that the auxiliary bishop will not reach Chongoyape today; so I spent the rest of the afternoon discussing the property problems of Monsefú with Bishop Figueroa and Father de la Rosa.

I returned home to find the electric power had been cut off; no more electricity for fifteen days. We were without power for three weeks last time; this time Chiclayo, too, is deprived. The Electric Company, when it functions, offers two kinds of service to Monsefú, 'domestic' which operates only at night, and 'industrial' which is a twenty-four hour service; but since the same transformers supply both services, the extra load at night causes so great a power drop that the motor of our refrigerator refuses to turn over. Efficiency is not a word that is highly prized down here.

MONSEFU, JULY 28TH, 1961

Father John Maddigan arrived a week ago tonight, accompanied by Father Tom Reilly. He just walked in as if he'd always been here; and Father Tom brought the good news that he himself might be able to stay for a couple of months while Father Maddigan is making his first acquaintance with the Spanish language. A day later Father John was laid low by one of the bugs that lie in wait for newly-arrived gringos. It hit him suddenly and hard and, remembering Dick Morse, I was very worried about him. However, he was on his feet again in a couple of days, chastened but otherwise none the worse for his experience. Food preparation is always suspect on such occasions, but I know that Dora who cooks for us and Simon who washes the dishes are very careful. But there is still the hazard of the dust that blows around.

Today, the most important day of the *Fiestas Patrias*, I was presented with a gold medal by the Municipal Council of Monsefú. The citation stated that I was being honoured 'for settling the religious problem'. The excommunicated

41

former mayor, now back in the arms of the Church, shared honours with me on the same grounds.

In the afternoon I listened to fifty or more little orators, one or two from each class of every school in town, all vocally fervent in their homage to their national flag, San Martin, and the heroes of Junin and of Ayacucho. Father John was not with me, which is just as well, as he might have felt humbled listening to toothless five-year-olds reciting with perfect confidence poems rich in refined subjunctives. One eleven-year-old boy has an altogether incredible range of expression. I predict that he'll be the leader of a political party some day.

Father John divides his time between Monsefú and the Vincentian College in Chiclayo where he will stay and where he will get his language study. He finds it hard to sleep here because of the bells which ring the hours in the clock tower of the church. The mechanism could easily be unhooked to cut off the sound during the night, but the Mayor tells me that the people for miles around time themselves by the bells in going to their fields, some as early as 3 a.m. I hope John will be able to adjust to this situation.

The Nonia sweater brought to me from home is a beauty, perfect in weight and warmth for our July mid-winter season. Somehow, I feel more competent when I have it on — like the soldier in the fairytale when he was wearing his seven-league boots. The black mood of discouragement and darkness of soul which overwhelms me at times is due, I think, to my awareness of being unequal to the job that has been laid upon me. At times this unhappiness will feed on almost anything — even on the kindness shown me and the disinterested help so generously given by others which I receive so readily and use so selfishly. St. Paul said that when he was weak, then he was strong. I suppose that can apply to anyone, but I find that an act of faith is no real solace to the feelings. Here I am, philosophizing myself into sadness when there is neither time nor need for it. I must get out and let the wind blow through me at a football game.

I drove down to Lima in Father Reilly's car, leaving him in charge of the parish, with John standing by. I am here to meet the London priests who arrived this morning at 5.45. I reached the airport forty minutes late, only to find that they had left in a taxi for parts unknown. I thought to my-self, "They know no Spanish; they don't know Lima; they don't even have the address of the Maryknollers where I have arranged for them to stay." I spent two unhappy hours on the phone, but that did me no good. Then they turned up on their own at 11 a.m. and I took them off to have lunch at the Nuncio's where I got quite a ribbing.

I'll have to call the newcomers Bill and Paul, as Cooney and Mooney sound too much like a music hall dance team. Bill is big, bright and athletic, with a good sense of humour. He is six years ordained. Paul is smaller, a little older and slight. He was ordained three years ago, one of four priest-brothers from the Windsor, Ontario, area. He was in the Air Force during the war and worked for some time before he went into the Seminary.

Later that day we visited the Villa Maria Convent to pick up a parcel of Spanish books for John Maddigan, leaving the car at the door. When we came out we found that the wing window had been jimmied open and Paul's flight bag, containing his breviary, glasses and pilot's licence had been stolen. We have put an advertisement in the paper and have some hope of getting the things back, as they are of little use to anyone else. Not so with my Nonia cardigan which was also taken.

Yesterday morning we went to the airport to meet Cardinal Cushing who was on his way to attend a Eucharistic Congress in a town in Bolivia which has been under martial law for the past week. Poor Bolivia! And today I had an interesting conversation with Juan Mejia Boca who oper-ates a book-store near the University. He is a native of Puerto Eten, not far from Monsefú. He is a friend of politi-cians and has been jailed seventeen times for expressing his

43

opinions. Yet he is no party man and, in all friendliness, tells the local statesmen that politics is of the stomach.

Monsefu, August 15th.

Father Michael Crowley was sent with me from Lima by Father Masciarelli, on whom all blessings descend! He is a Cork man who came with Cardinal Cushing to serve a three-year term with the St. James Society. He is fluent in Spanish, having worked for five years among the Puerto Ricans in New York.

We had a pleasant drive back from Lima, discussing profound and whimsical subjects. He sings Handel and old Gaelic songs, has a great sense of humour and a deep, simple charity. He is glad to be put so soon to work. He is indestructible, a gentle athlete who has won the confidence of the people with his friendly concern for the problems of the place.

On my return to Monsefú I found a letter waiting for me from Archbishop Skinner, inviting me to return to Newfoundland for a few weeks during September and October, so that I can help in the appeal for funds for our mission and can be present for the nuns' departure ceremony. So, we are to have our Mercy Sisters and our new presbytery. Father Mike feels sure the St. James Society will give him leave to remain here during my absence. I am beginning to suspect he may be the Archangel Michael in disguise.

Monsefu, September 15th

Father Maddigan is getting along well with his Spanish although he doesn't admit it. He claims that the dozen or more babies he baptizes every Sunday will never know how to pronounce their own names. He hears confessions now and has no trouble understanding or being understood, but he hasn't begun to preach yet.

44

Upper: A Bolivian religious holiday during one of Fr. Conroy's visits to Cocho-bamba. Lower: One of the bands at religious processions Fr. Conroy refers to.

Upper left: The Church of Monsefú with presbytery on right. Upper right: The statue of Señor Cautivo. Lower: Market scene before Monsefú Church in *fiesta* time.

I could not make plans to leave for Canada until after September 14th when our most important feast of the year is celebrated. No event in the life of the town is more important than the Feast of *El Senor Cautivo,* the Captive Lord. The hundred other feasts of the year are only pale reflections of the glory of that one.

The celebrations began officially on the evening of August 31st, at the railway station. The line is a narrow gauge one which runs through Monsefú from Chiclayo, ten miles north of the town, to Puerto Eten on the coast, five miles south. When the train came in that evening from Chiclayo, bringing no other passengers than a few High School students, crowds had gathered at the station. Meeting the train is the customary way of opening the Festival. There was great excitement when the first wailing of the *chirimia* was heard. This instrument is a reedy flute of penetrating pitch which assails the ear-drums mercilessly and, in the area around Chiclayo, is only used for this one feast. It is accompanied by a rapid drum-beat. The two musicians who were hired from nearby Marrope for the occasion scarcely stopped playing for the next two weeks.

At the station a parade formed and, accompanied by a band brought in from Jayanca and two bands from local schools, made its way to the park in front of the church. Fireworks enlivened the proceedings. As announced in the programme and reported afterwards, "The famous Monsefú pyrotechnician, Francisco Gonzales, launched into space his powerful rockets of triple detonation." On this point there was no exaggeration. Monsefú always sounds like a battlefield on festive occasions.

A dinner was served to the confraternity in charge of the celebration, and we sat down to peppered pigeon and boiled rice, with raw fish pickled in lime juice and giant kernels of sweet corn. Chica, the local brew, was available to cool the spice of the food.

The following days of the Novena, preparatory to the big feast, were quiet enough. We had the good fortune to have a Jesuit from Lima, Father Valdes, come to preach a mission. He has a great love of people, is gifted with a sense of humour and has no mercy on himself. Every day started at dawn with a procession through the streets, reciting the Rosary. Mass followed at 6.30, with a commentary by Father Valdes. During the day he talked to particular groups and organizations and each evening he preached to all. We had the Stations of the Cross outdoors one evening and Mass was offered in the cemetery another evening. "That's where the biggest part of the population of Monsefú is," was the comment of Father Valdez.

The Fiesta got going again with a bang on the 12th of September, when two bands marched around town competing with each other, the 'Pedro Ruiz Gallo' from the nearby town of Eten and the 'Carlos Gutierrez Noriega' of San Pedro de Lloc. At 6 a.m. next morning these two bands played their salute to the dawn, interrupted by what the programme termed 'sonorous detonations' of rockets of Peruvian and of Japanese style, while 'aerostatic globes' were sent aloft by a craftsman of the nearby countryside. These are six-foot-high paper kites, shaped rather like a chef's cap, panelled with paper of different colours. Waxed rope at the open end is ignited and generates enough heat to send them up several thousand feet, swinging towards Chiclayo in the southerly breeze. I don't know what a physicist would think of our space technicians, but no Monsefuano will ever be surprised by the news that someone has reached the moon.

That afternoon a new band arrived on the scene, hired by the Society of Farmers to compete with the two already mentioned. After Vespers in the church the serenading began, continuing all evening until, at midnight, the fireworks competition was held. The leader of one side was discouraged from calling his effort 'Up with the Grand Power of North America' as this was deemed politically embarrassing for his opponent. The contender from Chimbote, down the coast, had built a bamboo castle, fifty feet high, to hold his collection of 'lamps and brilliant showers of gilt and of silver; spinning wheels with green showers; pearls and brilliantines; strings of silver mosaico, greens, bright yellows, such as will make the sky bright, throwing off multicolours of golden stars.' It really was spectacular. To top it all off we had ten 'Pieces of Dessert', each with its title in the programme: 'Cascade', 'Sun Idol of the Incas', 'Flower of the Provinces', 'Bright Star', 'New Mirage', 'National Beauties', 'You see it and Don't Believe it', 'Butterfly's Flower', 'Glories of Peru' and 'Good Night'. It was 1 a.m. by this time, so we didn't wait for the local contender to make his response. It seemed, though, that he was hoping to impress the crowd with nuclear fission. The poor old house shuddered and we could smell brimstone.

The town was full of pilgrims, some from far-off mountain villages. They were different from our own people both in physical appearance and in their dress, more stolid and stocky in build and with faces that had a Tibetan quality. They put up stalls in the main square where they sold pottery, hand-woven materials and clothing, home-made biscuits and candy. Many of them slept in the open with no protection at all from the cold, September air.

The next morning, the day of the Feast, Bishop Figueroa came to preside at the Solemn Pontifical Mass. It was a joy to him to be warmly received by the very people he had been forced to excommunicate less than a year before. Father Maddigan and I had to fend off quite a few people who pushed against him in an effort to kiss his ring.

The statue of the Captive Lord was exposed for veneration during the days of the Feast in a chapel-hall adjoining the church. People stood in line for hours to approach it, kiss the feet or the chains hanging from the hands, bless themselves and sometimes pin paper money to the ribbon around the statue's shoulders. The society in charge of the feast receives in this way each year 80,000 soles, or about $3,200.00. Of the sum brought in about $2,400.00 is spent on the bands, fireworks, etc. $200.00 is sent to the diocesan seminary and the remaining $600.00 is spent on church projects in consultation with the parish priest. This small sum represents a third of the total income for the parish for the year. Although money goes farther here than it does in Canada, two thousand dollars is far from adequate for the running of a parish of twenty-one thousand people. The Monsefuanos are not accustomed to making generous dona-

47

tions because, in former times, the Church was supported by the government.

Sometimes gifts other than money are brought to The Captive Lord. One man tried to push his way through a line of devotos to present two new wigs of human hair which he wanted to try on the statue. I intervened, and he was lucky that I did not try them on him. Just the same, it was a glorious Feast.

I set off for Canada the next day, leaving the parish in good hands. There were further festivities in the days that followed, but the main celebration was over for another year. I was told by my companions to forget Monsefú for six weeks. Forget Monsefú!

MONSEFU, NOVEMBER 7, 1961

The place looked new and strange to me after my six weeks' absence, and I found everything well organized in the presbytery. The nuns have received a great welcome and are as merry as mice. An apartment has been put at their disposal in the Hacienda Pomalca while semi-permanent quarters are being looked for in the town for them. In January they will go to the Dominican nuns in Lambayeque and will remain with them until April when it is hoped their school quarters will be ready for them. During these months, while they are mastering the Spanish language, I am hoping to get their permanent convent started in Monsefú. Our own house is to be demolished soon, as our new presbytery is to be built on the same site. Things are bubbling here and we are busy and happy.

MONSEFU, NOVEMBER 24TH.

Father Maddigan has gone off to Lima to join the two London priests for the last weeks of their language study. Father Reilly has gone to his new parish in Talara and is settling in happily there; Father Crowley will remain with

48

me until the London men come, after which he will go to his new posting in Piura, the next town north of here.

I am having serious doubts about the wisdom of opening an English school in Chiclayo which will minister exclusively to well-to-do families, even though the object is to use the profits to meet the costs of maintaining a parish school in Monsefú. The Mercy Sisters could easily find themselves in the unhappy position of appearing to accept as right and natural an unjust social set-up which we all deplore, diminishing their effort to meet the really desperate need here in Monsefú. The Chiclayo School Committee is composed of well-to-do parents who are pressing for an English school for their children and its chairman is one of the two brothers who manage the Hacienda Pomalca. The Committee is inclined to force the issue. Father Crowley and I, however, feel that the Sisters have not a large enough staff to make a success of two schools. They must make their choice. Sister Mary Dorothy, the Superior, is in agreement with us and has written the Mother General of the Order in Newfoundland, putting the problem to her. If the final decision is to establish one school, and that in Monsefú, the burden of its support will lie heavily on the Order, as very little will come from the families of the children who will attend.

The longer I am in this country, the more I am struck by the sadness of the social set-up. In talking with rich people one can be charmed by the courtesy, the culture and the genuine humanity they exhibit but, whether they realise it or not, the well-to-do Peruvians, as a class, are exploiters. Many haciendas provide no schools for the thousands of families that are employed on them because, with even a little education, the people become restless.

MONSEFU, NOVEMRER 24TH.

Three priests of the St. James Society stayed with us last night, dropping in on their way north to open a parish in Negritos, near Talara. Before the new year is well under

49

way there will be twelve of them, most of them old friends of mine, working in and near Piura and in and near Talara, the two cities nearest to us to the north along the coast. Jack 'Ruthless' Thomas will be pastor at Negritos, with Jim Shanahan as curate; both are excellent men whom I know well. Mike Crowley who will go to Piura after Christmas will assist Paul Diebels, another friend of mine. Dave Kelly, an extraordinary young priest of tremendous zeal and talent will be pastor of the second parish in that town, and Larry Boudreau from Detroit will be his curate.

I am finding Mike not only delightful company but also a tireless worker. There are so many schools in this area and so great a number of children with uncertain parental backgrounds that preparing them for the sacraments is a very big undertaking. Still, we are managing it, with Mike doing more than a half share.

MONSEFU, DECEMBER 17TH.

We had a call from Lima this morning to tell Father Mike that Archdeacon Duggan of Cork had died there a few hours ago of a heart attack. He was an old man who, in his seventies, had resigned his parish and come to South America to join the St. James group. He was young at heart and thought nothing of undertaking a new language which he was well on the way to mastering. He explored Lima on foot, tramping everywhere without ever losing his way. He lived long enough after the attack to know that the end had come, and asked to be buried in Peru. Mike and two other priests from the Cork Diocese who are working in this area will leave for Lima tonight or tomorrow morning. Later in the week I am expecting the London priests, Bill Cooney and Paul Mooney, and of course John Maddigan will be with them.

The nuns have given up the idea of opening a school in Chiclayo, and thank God for that! Support from home was strong and definite in declaring for Monsefú only. It is a great relief to us all, and the nuns are happy to be free to devote themselves entirely to the parish here. The Chiclayo School Committee is understandably grieved about the decision but that wound should heal easily. In the meantime, the Sisters have left the Hacienda Pomalca and are now established in Chiclayo in a third-storey flat which will be their temporary convent.

MONSEFU, DECEMBER 21ST.

The team of Conroy, Cooney, Mooney and Maddigan is now complete, but we don't know how long it will remain that way. We hope to have the London priests with us for a year at least, but we know that pressure will be put on Bishop Cody of London, when he comes down here in a few weeks' time, to have his men take over a new parish as soon as they are ready for it, so urgent is the need in the Chiclayo Diocese. As things are developing around here, our own need is expanding all the time. We'll be hard put to it to manage if we are reduced in numbers.

Taking note of the Christmas season, we put on tape some excellent Spanish carols and played them through the outdoor speakers in the square in front of the church. It seems strange that I should never have heard the *villancicos* of Spain at Christmas time in Canada, although in recent years producers of radio and television programmes have been digging deep for Christmas themes. These Spanish carols are lovelier than most English ones I have heard.

The new year will open with the demolition of the presbytery. We are to take up living quarters in the government school across the square where we should be reasonably comfortable as there will be running water and plenty of space. The building will not be in use as a school until April as the long 'summer' holidays will last until then. The inversion of the seasons here below the equator is still a matter of wonder to me. The Sisters are entranced by it. The other day when their kettle announced it had reached boiling point by whistling, one of them said, "Will you listen to that wind! We won't get out the door this day for snow-drifts."

The Christmas season was busy and enjoyable and we found the local customs strange and interesting. There are the *pastorcitos* or little shepherds, small girls decked out in colourful finery who enter the church dancing and singing in monotonous voices, to the accompaniment of a harp, seventy or more verses of ancient Inca melodies in adoration of the *Niño Dios*, the Christ Child. I have on tape a snatch of the somewhat raucous voices of the little ones as they hopped and skipped and turned and sang their songs to Baby Jesus. It was hard work for them and perspiration gleamed on their small faces.

Other characters enter the scene at Christmas time also, clownish figures in costume who dance through the streets. Some are dressed as devils and carry whips or swords; some wear masks, often bigger than themselves, shaped like the heads of animals or ogres. An air of carnival prevails.

Although we priests did nothing to give a northern flavour to the Christmas Day festivities, the nuns somehow found a crib, a tree and a turkey and we all felt a little closer to home as a result.

We have undertaken a parish census — which entails visiting the homes of all the parishioners. Nearly every house, we find, possesses a statue, decked out in old velvet and a clutter of ornaments. One house I visited yesterday had a striking statue of St. John of God: a gaunt, grey face with intense gaze fixed on the ceiling of the little room, where he lay behind a broken-down barber's chair in the corner, wrapped in a dirty shirt. The statue, which had come from the oldest church in Chiclayo, recently pulled down, had been hollowed out by termites. Nevertheless the family are about to increase their poverty by getting elaborate and expensive vestments for St. John.

We have put our jeep at the disposal of the Sisters, since we have the use of the Scout car-truck provided by the Diocese of London, Ontario, and Father John's motor scooter as well. Every morning they drive from Chiclayo to round up the children and, next week, they will open a refectory which will provide breakfast daily for two hundred children between the ages of two and five whose parents cannot give them suitably nourishing food. The makings of the breakfast, powdered milk and flour for bread, come from the National Catholic Relief Service of the United States; the small cost of preparing it will be met by donations from our own people in Monsefú.

The old presbytery was abandoned on January 3rd and next day demolition was begun. We are enjoying the brightness of our new quarters. We each have a spacious classroom to sleep in, except Father Cooney who occupies the stage of the little auditorium. Looking for the limelight, we tell him.

After we had settled in we all returned to the old house and stood on the three-feet-thick walls with the workers, swinging picks and shovels for a couple of hours, tumbling down the adobe bricks. The dust rose for miles, and blisters soon appeared on soft hands; but we got some good exercise and we made a point firmly — that we are not fastidious foreigners, living above and away from the people, but are deeply involved in all that concerns the parish.

The new presbytery which will be begun almost at once will be rectangular in shape, built around a central patio which will be skirted by a covered walk like a cloister. The part at the rear of the patio will be of heavy enough construction to take a second storey if it is ever needed. The building will be of brick with concrete facing and reinforced concrete beams and pillars. It will have five bedrooms and three offices, one of which will be large enough to hold a meeting of up to thirty people; there will be a little chapel in which to reserve the Blessed Sacrament, a large recreation room, small dining-room, kitchen, pantry and store-room. And there will be plumbing. The cost will be about $15,000.

We are hoping to be able to occupy our new home when we vacate the school quarters in April. The Sisters will move to Monsefú at that time to occupy a house which a local doctor and his wife are making available to them for a few months, until their convent is ready. It is to be built in the field on the edge of town, owned by the parish — the site chosen by Reverend Mother Imelda and Sister Dorothy last June.

We were all shocked and saddened by the news, last week, of the Huarascaran catastrophe which occurred a couple of hundred miles to the south-east of us, when three million tons of glacial ice roared down the face of that great mountain and buried seven small settlements and most of their inhabitants, sparing only about three hundred of the four thousand people of the area. Since then we have been saddened by a man-made tragedy much closer to ourselves, though infinitesimal in scope if we think in terms of numbers. It happened in the Hacienda Pomalca which is a state-within-a-state, as are so many of the great haciendas which provide so much luxury for the few and so much less than subsistence for the many in this land of ancient privilege and oppression. Eight people were killed there yesterday, including a three-year-old child, and seventy injured, when the Assault Guard of the hacienda, stationed there because of perennial labour troubles, opened fire on strikers who were seeking recognition of their union as their legal bargaining agent. The workers, having no strike funds to support their families during the walk-out, were growing desperate in their attempts to force an interview with the management.

Most of the haciendas in this area resist unionization with firm, though benign rule; but Pomalca, which employs about fifteen thousand people, has established a policy of relying on force.

A few days ago we had a visit from Canon Boulart of the Archdiocese of Paris, an elderly French priest who has helped to co-ordinate the work of religious orders, diocesan clergy and the laity in about fifty dioceses throughout the world. He came more to inquire than to inform, but afterwards we had much to discuss. The deviation from the Church's ideal is so marked here and there is so strong a tide in daily life that brings about a drift away from religion, that it is difficult for the individual to feel that he can do much about it. Canon Boulart thinks that the effects of the terrible shortage of priests in Latin America could be mitigated by closer unity among those who are here, together with certain carefully-planned changes in policy. He believes that small-scale projects, implementing the social teaching of the popes, would do much to stem the tide of secularism. He thinks our team of four priests is ideal.

He asked how we divide the work. I couldn't lay a very detailed plan before him because our full complement only came together in time for Christmas and in the interval we had moved house. Still, there is a pattern. Father John Maddigan goes every morning to Santa Rosa, five miles from Monsefú over a bad road, where he is taking a parish census. He finds the people there amiable and cooperative, but hardly Catholic in any recognizable sense of the word. He looks after the Legion of Mary there and the men's group recently organized to take care of repairs to the chapel. He is also making plans to start a Credit Union which will meet a much felt need in the parish and which will manifest the social teachings of the Church. In addition he looks after the accounts of the house. Father Bill Cooney is responsible for Callanca, a farming community of about thirty-four hundred people, about the same size as Santa Rosa in numbers, but more spread out in area. It is about eight miles from Monsefú in a different direction. He is also planning a young men's group here in the heart of the parish. Father Paul Mooney has a fine Legion of Mary under his care and is forming an altar boys' society, the 'Little Clergy', as they call it here. I am supposed to be looking after the rest — period!

Canon Boulart had with him a young Canadian from Lima, a priest of the Montreal Foreign Mission Society, and also a Peruvian priest who is pastor of a slum parish on the outskirts of Lima, but whose family is one of the forty who are said to own Peru. We went, today, to visit a hacienda owned by this family and, although it is the best of all the factory farms around these parts, as far as living and working conditions are concerned, yet the management is paternalistic, and there is no union.

It is interesting to observe a reform in the way of thinking that is developing in a new generation in Peru. This young priest feels keenly the absence of social conscience in his otherwise good family. His brother, who is the author of a paper on social justice which the hierarchy of Peru saw fit to publish as a joint pastoral letter some years ago, has become something of a family outcast as a result.

MONSEFU, FEBRUARY 15, 1962

We have had a busy time of it since Canon Boulart's visit. He gave a week of conferences in Lima which I attended with three other priests from this diocese. I was there when Bishop Cody of London arrived, in company with a papal knight, Robert Williams, who is vice-president of the St. Vincent de Paul Conferences in Canada. I took him out that afternoon in a borrowed car on a visit to Pampa de Comas, a squatters' slum suburb of Lima, where eighty thousand people have settled in the past five years. The Canadian Oblates look after the parish there as well as they can with a three-man team, one of whom is a new-comer on the scene. On the way back we ran over some glass and by the time we reached the hotel where Bishop Cody was waiting for us, one of the tires was down. A taxi-driver outside the hotel looked after it for us but refused payment when he learned that we had come from a visit to the priests at Pampa de Comas where he lives. This gracious act was his personal salute to the Canadian Oblates whom he greatly admires.

Bishop Cody had allowed himself only a week for his high-speed pastoral visit to his mission in South America. He was determined not to waste a minute of it, particularly as his plane had arrived late and had already deprived him of half a day. That evening we all dined at the Nunciature where, afterwards, he and the Nuncio had a long private talk about the work to be done. Early next morning we were on our way to Chiclayo by plane and after he had said Mass in the cathedral there we took him to the one good hotel in town for lunch and afterwards to Monsefú. Later in the afternoon the bishop made a tour of the parish, or all of it that can be reached by road and, in the course of it, got one involuntary whiff of a dumping area where clouds of flies swarmed into the car.

During his short stay among us the Bishop went into the Chiclayo slums, visited the lovely church in Lambayeque, managed things so that his own men, Father Bill and Father Paul, were able to have long sessions with him, spent an afternoon at a hacienda which is unique in that the social ideals of the Church appear to be fully realised there. He found there a good community spirit, personal freedom, a strong union, good working conditions and wages, including a sharing in profits, and wise social fringe benefits. In addition, credit and consumer co-operatives are encouraged among the workers. Before he left he invited us all out to dinner at the hotel in Chiclayo in company with Bishop Sanchez-Moreno, Father Fernandez, the chancellor of the diocese and Robert Williams.

On Saturday morning Bishop Cody flew back to Canada where other bishops are gathering to greet him on the twenty-fifth anniversary of his consecration. He brought back with him a few straw mats as souvenirs of his visit and also, I think, a very clear idea of conditions down here and a full awareness of our circumstances and needs. I got the impression of a very alert mind, not easily confused by detail. In spite of age and illness, he exhibited such unflagging energy that he left us all exhausted.

Robert Williams is interested in founding branches of the St. Vincent de Paul Conferences down here, as our friends, the priests from St. Louis, Mo. have already done with great success in La Paz, Bolivia. I think I'll holler for a dispensary. He says he thinks St. Vincent de Paul might help.

In the indirect apostolate we already have definite plans for a credit union. We have arranged for the sale of a large piece of church land to a group of young men who have had 4-H training. Through them these two hundred and fifty acres can be redeveloped scientifically, to the benefit of the community, with the co-operators studying the project thoroughly first and paying off the cost of the land over a twenty year period. And there are other ideas too — the training of a lay apostolate, for instance, which would be self-perpetuating through its leadership. But there are also other urgencies which are too demanding on our time and energies to permit us to wander down dream by-paths.

MONSEFU, MARCH 11TH, 1962

Santa Rosa is giving us trouble at the moment. We have been trying to unify the groups there and get some control of their activities — but they are having none of it. The four societies which look after the celebrations of the Feast of Our Lady of Mount Carmel there got together last month and, without telling us anything about it, arranged to have an altar made in the chapel for their statue of Our Lady. When we refused it, by announcement made at Mass on Sunday, pointing out that until the most badly needed repairs to the chapel are completed no other undertakings will be approved, the mayordomos of the various societies got up and walked out. They claimed that Father Maddigan was trying to make Protestants of them. Certainly, as far as recognizing any authority in the Church is concerned, they are already that. Father John, who was distressed by the incident, takes a little comfort in the thought that he has an excellent committee who are pledged to put the chapel in good repair.

The Mercy Sisters, who have been with the Dominican nuns in Lambayeque for the past three months, are getting ready to move to Monsefú. They will occupy Dr. Custodio's house until they can move into their convent which is not even begun yet.

The parish house is rising rapidly, in spite of man-made delays. We are waiting now for materials, including iron for the windows of house, church and chapel, which are being brought to us by truck from Lima. But the bridge over the Viru River, between here and Lima has, for long-time lack of repair, become too dangerous to bear the weight of trucks, five hundred of which are waiting to cross on their way north. Acts of God in the legal sense are not the only cause of disaster in this country. I doubt if anything less momentous than the collapse of the Viru bridge under the weight of a frustrated truck or bus is likely to bring action in this case.

MONSEFU, MARCH 26TH.

This morning two, or maybe three Mothers General from Ontario are expected, and perhaps one from Mexico City. They will be on a tour of investigation of the school situation in this area. With all this there should soon be a settlement of the Chiclayo school problem, although I am now so disgusted with the social injustice on all sides of us that I could savagely hope the exclusive school never comes into being. However, I would be prepared to concede the need for one with a broad base and a firm policy of making the children of wealthy families aware of social problems and ready to face up to them. The recent tragic occurrence at the Hacienda Pomalca is not an isolated incident. Only very recently, in the high mountains, some Indian communities, driven by need, settled overnight on one of the huge estates and, in 'Operation Dislodgement', many were killed and injured by the police.

With the Feast of St. Joseph this month we begin to say good-bye to summer. In our fishing community of Santa Rosa it is the most important feast of the year, bringing people all the way from Chiclayo who come by way of our neighbouring parish of Pimentel, walking over the fifteen miles of good asphalt road. During the feast celebrations the statue of St. Joseph in the Santa Rosa chapel is given a silver

59

crown to wear, replacing the to us incongruous straw hat which is its year-round headgear. This year the mayordomos of the Feast have been more than anxious to have the Captive Lord statue from Monsefú visit Santa Rosa to give importance to the Feast, as happened last year in thanksgiving for the safety of the little town from destruction in the disastrous tidal wave of 1960. This year we held firm against all petitions and turned a deaf ear to the interminable arguments in favour of the proposal. In spite of the fact that our refusal was unqualified, the program was printed without change from its original form and the mayordomos made a last-minute attempt to force us into conformity. They pointed out how highly educated we were and how ignorant they were themselves; how nice it would be if we would give them time to learn the fine points of ecclesiastical discipline — and could the Captive Lord come, as he was the star feature of their celebration? Again the answer was No.

MONSEFU, APRIL 12TH, 1962

The other day Father Paul Mooney, who holds a pilot's licence, took me up for a spin among the clouds in a borrowed private plane. The only danger we felt we had to guard against was from buzzards, as these creatures fly pretty high and are big enough to be a hazard if they happen to be on collision course with a light plane. And, of course, we were careful to pick a time when there were no rockets soaring up from the town. It was a thrilling feeling to see the whole parish spread out below us. I took a series of pictures of Monsefú and Santa Rosa, only to discover later that the film had caught in the sprocket and had not been turning. The hardest penances to bear, I find, are not the ones that are imposed by the Divine Will, nor the ones deliberately chosen, but are those that result from one's own stupidity. I do not undertake any of the second variety because the first and third are imposed on me often enough to keep me in my place.

The airport in Chiclayo is jointly controlled by the civil and military authorities. Father Paul had not been told that, having no radio, he was expected to buzz the control tower for permission to land. We were circling to come down when he realised with a shock that two Canberra jet bombers were roaring in for a landing at the same time, just ahead of us. There was no time for him to change course, so the jets were forced to overfly us and circle around again to come in for a second try. As a result of all this there was a spectacular row between the civil and Air Force authorities, while the man who had lent us the plane narrowly missed losing his licence. The incident, we learned, was only one of many causes of grievance between the two authorities. We never did learn what the other grievances were as we were too chastened by the experience to ask questions.

The Perils of a P.P. did not end with the sky-ride. I think I hold a record for being perforated by a sting-ray and splashed by a vulture all in the same week. The ray was flapping about near some rocks on the floor of the ocean when I went in for a swim. I inadvertently stepped on the creature and got three punctures in the sole of my foot. It was a painful experience which, after several days of limping about, sent me to a hospital in Chiclayo for treatment. The Sister who examined my badly swollen foot told me that the people on the coast, if stung by a ray, kill the creature and remove the entrails which they then apply to the affected part. Even if I had been versed in folk medicine, as she apparently was, I doubt if I would have been willing to attempt to kill a sting-ray with my bare hands. I was quite satisfied to make do with antibiotics and a lemon juice rub.

The vulture took me unawares. It was sitting on the south tower of the church when I came through the big front doors. Since the wind blows always from the south, and the moment was unfortunate, my pastoral dignity was a little dampened. I had to wash off my glasses before I could see again.

Today I went on an outing with three of the priests of the Chiclayo Diocese to Tembladera, a town in the neighbouring Diocese of Cajamarca. The young parish priest there has made a hobby of gold-plating by electrolysis, so

61

we brought him several chalices that were in need of re-gilding. But the excursion was chiefly for pleasure, and it turned out to be a very enjoyable one.

It is always very hot in Tembladera which nestles in a valley between high mountains. It is the first parish inland from the coast on the road that winds high over the cor-dillera or mountain ridge to Cajamarca, site of the capture and execution of Atahualpa, the last of the Inca emperors. Father Ugaz has been there with his parents for the past three years. It is encouraging to see the numbers of fine young priests there are in these areas, in spite of all ob-stacles and difficulties. In most parts of the country the lack of schools is the chief of several serious drawbacks to the en-couragement of vocations to the priesthood, and it seems close to miraculous that even a few should get through to be ordained.

In spite of the poverty of Father Ugaz' parish we were treated to a Peruvian meal that went on endlessly and when we left he refused to accept any remuneration for the gild-ing.

On the way back we drove into one of the most beautiful sunsets I have ever seen, with a great rainbow, arching from the top of a mountain on our left and the flaming sky ahead reflected in the water of the rice fields and glowing through the fresh greenery. We stopped on the way to visit an old, retired priest of the diocese who is known as a healer. He told us that the good results he gets come mainly from his knowledge of herbal medicine which is a hobby of his, al-though he admitted to a certain intuitive ability to diagnose which appears to be a gift of nature.

We have little hope of getting into our new home before the end of May, so we continue to occupy the auditorium of the Government school which is now in session. At least we have no reason to complain regarding lack of co-opera-tion on the part of the teachers.

The sisters moved into Dr. Custodio's house the last week of March and are now busily coping with a hundred and thirty children in the chapel-hall beside the church which has been partitioned for two classes of Grade I and one of

Grade II. The hall will serve as a school for this year at least. Eventually we hope to have a school building which will adjoin the Sisters' convent on the Las Animas property at the edge of town — but first we must get the convent built. It is to be a gift from all the Convents of Mercy in Newfoundland. For the present the Sisters are merry pioneers, grateful for the shelter of the small, three-room adobe house which will be their home for the next few months.

MONSEFU, MAY 29TH, 1962

We have been very busy lately with Confirmations which are not easy to organize. There is a great deal of paper work to be attended to in connection with them and much time must be given to instruction as well as to hearing hundreds of confessions. We held the ceremony last Thursday, and all went well. Although about a hundred were missing who should have been present, all who came showed quiet reverence. The scene was very different from the hurly-burly in evidence in the parishes where there is one lone Peruvian priest and no home guard. Even in our church it is not always easy to keep control; the dogs of the parish often seem surprised and pained when their presence at the altar is questioned.

I am trying to keep a firm hand while wearing a velvet glove, but I lost the glove one day recently when I lifted and shoved a drunk out of the church at the close of a fiesta celebration. Peruvians seldom give overt expression to anger and seem more amused than impressed when they see it in others; so maybe it wouldn't help to knot a cord, as Our Lord did in the Temple. I was raging that day, but in a controlled and directed way, just energetic and determined-like. And it worked.

The early Spanish missionaries seem to have implanted in the Peruvian Indian a great devotion to Our Lord in his suffering, but did not follow through with an understanding of the joy of the saints or the glory of the Resurrection. And over centuries of unconquered ignorance, the pagan spirit of an earlier culture crept into the penitential feasts and made them joyful in the wrong way, characterized by drunken disorders. The faith, growing ever more superficial became overlaid by superstition; yet, the instinct of the people remained Christian.

We are beginning to move into our new home by inches. Only the bedrooms are ready yet, but the finishing won't take many more weeks and, even at this stage it is a joy to us to find ourselves at least partially in possession. In the meantime we are deeply appreciative of the whole-hearted generosity of the school authorities in permitting us to take up residence in the Government school for all these months while our new home was being built.

It is good, too, to be able to report that the Sisters' convent will be under way any day now. We received the plans from the architect a couple of weeks ago and, after several busy and interesting days and nights spent in working out comparisons in the figures of five competing engineers who sent in tenders for the construction, were happy to give the contract to Engineer Paz who has built the new presbytery and with whom we have had very happy dealings.

Best news of all is that the Newfoundland team is to be increased to three with the arrival in a few weeks' time of Father Jim Doody who is giving up a prosperous parish to come down here with us. The London men, Father Bill and Father Paul, will remain with us for a while longer, but will eventually take on the large parish of Cayalti-Zana which, in the meantime, will be under our combined care.

Elections are in preparation and excitement is growing in the town. We had a visit from a Communist priest recently — not to us personally, but for a political rally which turned out to be a flop. The Communists have candidates on every party's list, as they have no hope of winning any victories on their own. Our one and only official Monsefú Communist is a candidate for the Senate; he gets a pension from Moscow and spends part of it helping with the costs of the fiesta celebrations.

The official Communist line does not attack the Church, wisely refraining because the country is so Catholic in its customs and in its loyalties. A good example of their wolf-in-sheep's-clothing approach is a complaint made by one of them recently in the Bishop's residence that the priests in Monsefú interfered and would not let them hold a peaceful demonstration. Actually, we had ignored the meeting and had even dealt firmly with a young man of one of the rival parties who tried to ring the church bells during the meeting in the hope of starting a fight. Father Maddigan claims he had even sympathised with one of the visiting Communists, saying, "Too bad you had such a poor attendance. It must be discouraging to find out that there are so many thousands of people in this town who haven't even a curiosity interest in you."

As election fever mounts, our town grows noisier. One of the politicians up for re-election came here last week with a band of minstrels to orchestrate his show. Not a day passes but trucks and cars go by, blaring on loud-speakers or beating themselves on their tin chests and shouting a victory that is still in the future for one candidate or another. Father Mooney tells me I had better watch out because, if I pause in a meditative moment in the street, as I sometimes do, I may be plastered with posters. Last week two huge cases from Sweden which were unloaded in the street opposite the town hall, were completely covered by evening with pictures and slogans. The cases are supposed to contain the pumps for the water system which the town is supposed to enjoy. I'll know more about that when they are moved from the street to the house that was supposed to have been built to contain them near the elevation tank which is still in the planning stage.

Inquiries from Canada indicate concern about the political situation down here and the possibility of revolution. We are not worried about any such development, although the country seems to be asking for it in many ways. The coming election is almost sure to be peaceful, but if the new government does nothing to dispel the cynicism — I might almost say the despair — that is the feeling of most people, revolution within the next few years is a possibility.

While fear of violence gives us no concern at the present time, we are not exempt from a type of mental suffering which is so subtle that words to describe it do not come easily. The refinement of torture which produces it has been developed in Peru over a period of many centuries. I offer a very simple example:

You, the victim, wish to get a driver's licence. You find the licensing office in Chiclayo; you wait in line; you are told the application must be made on official state paper, with tax stamps, neither of which can be furnished in that office. You return another day bringing the application, and are told that you must take a medical test. You are given the name of the official doctor who is authorised to make the examination — no other will satisfy the requirements — and you leave to seek him out. But you find he is hard to track down. It takes two weeks to get the medical which is given in two sections, each of which tests the victim's patience more than his motor reflexes or his general physical fitness. Two or three more visits to the licensing office are required to find out what the next hurdle is; you are directed to the person in charge of driving tests, but it takes several calls on him before he has time to arrange the test; and when he does, you find the course is designed by the devil — up a cliff and over sideways, without a road or a clue as to where the front wheels of the vehicle are heading for. If you have a jeep and use four-wheel drive from the start, you win the test, but when you go to the office later you find the report has not been turned in yet. When you call back another day you find that the photographs you presented in satisfaction of the requirements are not the right size, and that in the profile the left side should be showing and not the right. This is remedied and, two weeks later, the tax stamps are acquired and you find the papers are in order. But this is not the end. The Director of Transport is in transit somewhere and the temporary licence cannot be signed until his return. You lick your wounds while you are waiting. The permanent licence is delayed because it must come from Lima and there is a shortage there of the plastic that is used to protect licences. So, each month you must check at the licensing office to have your temporary permit renewed. The Director may happen to be there and, if he is not too busy, will sign the renewal. Then, in ten months' time the permanent licence arrives — unless it is lost, as Mike Crowley's was.

NEGRITOS, JUNE 14, 1962

I have been away from Monsefú for five days and am writing this in Negritos, near Talara, in one of the St. James Society stations. Father Paul Diebels, on his way back to Piura from Lima, stopped over in Monsefú, and I went on with him, staying two days in his parish before coming on here. I was not needed on Sunday because Masses were cancelled by government and episcopal decree between 8 a.m. and 6 p.m. The reason — the voting for a new president. Voting was heavy and peaceful, but the results are not clear yet. It is a close race between Belaunde and Haya de la Torre, with the old dictator, Odria, an uncomfortably competitive third. The National Assembly will probably have to make the decision because candidates of four splinter parties make it dificult for the winner to have the required one-third of the total vote.

It is good to sleep in and have nothing pressing to do. I would like to get better organized in our own parish work, as scattering of effort leaves us always on the edge of worry. Now, with the new parish of Cayalti under our care, and with the London priests anxious to get at it, it is difficult to plan a program for our own parish. It will be easier when Father Doody is with us and 'linguafied'.

I am reading Teilhard de Chardin's 'The Divine Milieu' which says in many words that the unreconciled dualism in the minds of men between matter and spirit, or nature and grace, is unfortunate, because all the natural needs, all the evolution of creation, are connected with the divine life which God wants for us. A Christian, he feels, cannot be half-hearted in his attitudes about the things of this world without opposing God's plan. I must appear as vague and

67

floundering as I thought he was; but in spite of the fact that the book is in translation and is full of afterthoughts and footnote clarifications, it is one which reaches to fundamentals and has been very helpful to me. It is a book which makes one realise better what one already knew intuitively, but without enough assurance for it to be a basis for action.

Mike Crowley and another Irishman, Father Pat Lohan from Galway, are curates under Paul Diebels in Piura, but the parish is new and is composed of a mixed bag of very different neighbourhoods that are without any natural common ties. And there are a number of schools and religious communities working in the same area that are doing much of the necessary work, though they are not technically responsible for the parish. While Father Diebels is getting his church built in Piura, the two Irishmen will probably move out to look after one of the many huge, poor and abandoned country parishes, as they feel they are being wasted at the moment. And they have only been allowed leave from their home diocese in Ireland for a maximum of three years.

The social problems of this country are given grim emphasis in Piura where economic injustice is extreme, as evidenced by badly paid and completely dependent workers. Mike says he didn't come to South America to make things easier for the wealthy. He is prepared, though, to help them indirectly by organizing unions and other undertakings which should satisfy some of their obligations to their fellow creatures. Paul Diebels agrees with Mike, although he is inclined to think that he is still fighting the British. It would be hard not to agree, because Mike is the most convincing debater you ever could meet. He is just a bit beyond most of us in vision, and he is very sound. He is largely responsible for our coming to a firm decision in the Chiclayo school question.

Speaking of social problems, 'Time' magazine published an article recently on Pope John's encyclical letter, 'Mater et Magister' and on how it is being implemented in Latin America. With the sort of sly, off-hand remark they specialise in, they say that a bishop in Sao Paolo, Brazil, joined the picket lines with his people in a labour dispute and used his fists like a veteran on strike breakers. Perhaps something like this could happen in Sao Paolo, with its military traditions; but in Peru the hierarchy tries to improve situations by personal influence, giving no offence to anyone. Peruvians never want to see one person hurting another directly. They leave it to 'things' to do the damage, mostly by neglect. But the ecclesiastical attitude is not effective, and the males of the country came to look down on the clergy for never taking a strong stand. It is a repeating pattern of world history. I keep wondering if history can be diverted from its course by those who have learned its lessons and, if so, how many lessons and how many learners there would have to be to produce effect.

MONSEFU, JULY 3RD, 1962

Father Jim Doody will arrive in Lima next week. I plan to be there to meet him, as I have other business to see to there which can be arranged for that time. He will attend the small language school outside the city which the St. James Society has formed and will be there until the end of October. A friend sent me an item of news from one of the Newfoundland papers which read, "Rev. James Doody, former Catholic priest from Oderin, P.B., will leave shortly for Peru." I wrote him, assuring him he would be as welcome as if it weren't true.

MONSEFU, JULY 20TH, 1962

The results of the elections in Peru are a surprise to no one. Allegations of fraud and demands for a recount began to grow loud as it became apparent, even before the last ballots were counted, that it was to be a very close race, with a majority of the popular vote going to Haya de la Torre. Twice before, he and his American Popular Revolutionary Alliance (known as APRA) had been prevented from coming into power by the strength of military influence. Yesterday a Military Junta took over the Government, promising another election soon. We shall have to wait to find out what will happen.

Jim Doody arrived on schedule and, if the supreme authority had been vested in me, would have been welcomed with a twenty-one gun salute. As it was, Father Masciarelli of the St. James Society and I were at the airport to greet him. The next two days were spent showing him around the lovely city of Lima. He was particularly interested in the tour we made of the beautiful old church and cloister where the recently canonized St. Martin de Porres lived and served God and his fellow men. Curiously enough, although Peruvians are both nationally conscious of and fervently devoted to the saints, St. Martin, in recent times, has been better known outside than inside his own country. His canonization, however, has aroused great interest and renewed devotion. An excellent Spanish movie, 'Brother Broom', depicting his life, was released simultaneously in all parts of Peru at the time of the canonization. The Government declared 1962 'The Year of Fray Martin', a phrase which is to be placed at the head of all official documents.

Fray Martin is by no means the first Negro canonized. Being of mixed blood and being noted for his justice and charity, he is a good champion of social justice. Unlike Father Bartolome de las Casas, a priest of his time, who was a champion of the emancipation of the slaves, Martin modestly suggested to his own superior at a time when the community was sadly in need of funds, that Brother Martin might bring a fair price if sold into slavery. His attendance on the sick, the poor, the persecuted, and even his humourous kindness to animals, were the lesson that savage age needed most of all. He presides now as patron over works of mercy in all parts of the world.

Later that day we called at the Monsefú Club, the membership of which is composed of Monsefuanos living and working in Lima, and were invited to return for a meeting that evening. We also visited the Columban Fathers in the Rimac river-bed, where Father Jim was surprised and delighted to meet Father Sean Morrissey who had been at the seminary with him in Dublin.

In the evening, at about 9.30, we returned to the Monsefú Club to attend the meeting called for 8 o'clock and found ourselves the first arrivals. Soon afterwards the members came drifting in. As each one entered, he touched a picture of the statue of the Captive Lord, blessed himself and deposited an alms for the coming great September feast. Then each Monsefuano, young or old, courteously greeted every person in turn, and the meeting was called to order. After business matters had been got out of the way, the birthday of the vice-president was celebrated with speech and counter-speech; libation followed libation, each touching off a salvo of exuberant praise for the *Padres Canadienses* and fresh expressions of fervent homage to the picture of the Captive Lord. At midnight we made a strategic retreat, leaving the meeting still in full glow.

Father Jim's second day in Lima began with a visit to Father Sean Morrissey's parish on the 'Monton', a section of the great garbage dump of the city, where five thousand people live, and many other creatures as well. Thousands of pigs could be counted pushing through the piles of burning rubbish, and a score of dogs came snapping at the car from every alley we passed. For all the squalor there was an air of hope in the area. The rough little chapel which held the Blessed Sacrament was quiet inside; we looked in at a library and a school, both of which were functioning normally. We found Father Sean giving instructions as to what was to be done with two thousand bricks which had just been dumped near the school.

We were invited to lunch by the Columban Fathers and, while commemorating the Glorious Twelfth, prayed for rain in Belfast. That evening we had supper at the Nunciature, as Archbishop Carboni wanted to meet Father Doody. We

71

went afterwards with the Nuncio to a play, 'The King's Postman' by Rabindranath Tagore, in the Seminary of St. Toribio where seminarian performers showed extraordinary skill in acting and equal ability in devising settings for this difficult production. Father Jim says that when he knows enough Spanish he intends to go back there to tell them how much he enjoyed the performance.

The following day we visited the language school of the St. James priests where Jim will take up his Spanish studies, in company with twenty other priests. The surroundings are quiet and beautiful, a verdant valley set down among burnt and naked mountains. The next morning we boarded the plane for Chiclayo. In the days before the opening of the language school he will have an opportunity of learning something about the parish and the people of Monsefú and the size of the undertaking that lies ahead of him.

MONSEFU, LATER, SAME DAY.

This is being written in semi-darkness, with a candle perched beside me on a box of flea powder Father Doody brought me. We are to be without electricity at night for the next week at least, but are soon to get a portable generator which will make us a little independent of the vagaries of the local system. A couple of months ago, while we were suffering similarly, I happened to meet the Company engineer who is in charge of the area, in the town of Reque where I had been invited to give a Sunday sermon. I asked him why we were being penalised. He told me the town of Monsefú owed the Company $4,000.00 for its public light; that the power line along the railway track was old and worn and another transformer was needed, but the Company in Lima refused to lay out money for equipment in an area that is so desperately poor-paying. Moreover, a generator in Chiclayo was out of order and the needed part had not yet been flown from England. It looks as though all these good reasons are still applicable.

I have examined the container which serves as a stand for my candle and note the directions on it: 'Dust entire dog, beginning at the head and working back.' It also says, 'Dust dog's living quarters freely.' But I can't waste such precious stuff over such a large area. I had written Father Jim, telling him something of living conditions down here and had confessed that I would like to borrow a little flea powder from some dog — but that I didn't have any dog friends down here. His gift has the disadvantage of being a purple powder but any resemblance between the user and an ancient Briton would be purely coincidental.

Father Maddigan leaves on holiday in three days' time. I had intended to wait until January for my holiday, but have been counselled, as I wanted to be, to join Father Mike Crowley on a tour in the countries to the south of us. We would both like to know what is happening in these countries, and Mike would be a marvellous companion. Wherever we go he will find grist for his mill. As I mentioned earlier, he is a born debater, but he doesn't at all mind having an opponent who takes up little if any of the talking-time. I very much enjoy and profit by his lectures, especially on pastoral theology and psychology, Gaelic literature and song, European economics, agriculture, bee culture, and human nature in all its aspects. He is an extraordinary person. There can be nothing better in Ireland.

The first results of the military take-over of power are being seen already. Soldiers are stopping all cars at thirty-mile intervals along the coast road. There seems no mood for revolution, although I suppose it could build up. July 28th, the anniversary of independence, could be a dangerous date.

MONSEFU, JULY 23RD.

Over the weekend we made the major move into the new presbytery. When the refrigerator, all the furniture and the parish books were brought across and put in place we felt that at last we had a home of our own. The clean brightness of the house, with its tiled floors and spacious common-room, is a joy. The out-door covered walk, skirting an inner court-yard with garden space, gives us a privacy which is a rare privilege down here where, even at the altar during the celebration of the Holy Sacrifice, the parishioners feel free to approach any of us on matters of personal concern.

The convent is at last going up in the *Las Animas* ten-acre field. It will be a quiet and beautiful building on the edge of our dirty, noisy, ugly town. There are problems, however. The fetid irrigation ditch which runs between the property and the town presents a health hazard. There is a proposal to run a tree-lined road down the course of the ditch, but the scheme would leave the ditch on the nuns' side of the new road, and to divert it elsewhere would be too costly for easy accomplishment.

The Sisters, although working under difficulties in make-shift school quarters, have added more than a hundred and fifty children in evening classes to the school enrollment, bringing the total to close to three hundred. The evening-school classes, lasting for about an hour and a half, five days a week, are for children from eight to twelve years of age who have had no previous schooling.

It has been the experience of the Maryknoll priests and, in fact, of all who have worked in Latin America, that the best way to revive a parish is through schools conducted by nuns. We have already proved the truth of this here in Monsefú. But the Sisters do not stop with their school ef-fort. They also visit the families of the town; they direct the catechists who come to give Sunday afternoon instruc-tions and they have undertaken to direct catechetical in-struction in our neighbouring parish of Eten; they have charge of the sacristy in our church in Monsefú and have expressed their willingness to administer a dispensary which we are thinking of opening, with co-operation from local doctors.

Now it is Sunday morning, and John Maddigan will take off for Lima this afternoon. I am hoping he will manage to get a flight out tomorrow, but there is some reason for wor-ry, as a general strike has been called which may cripple transportation. He plans to be away for only two Sundays, although that seems to me to be too short a time to be worth the expense and difficulties of a journey to Newfoundland and back.

MONSEFU, AUGUST 16TH.

The murder in Bolivia of a Maryknoll friend of mine, Bill Kreuger, has overshadowed all other concerns. I met him first in Cochabamba and, later, on two separate visits to Lima, grew to feel great respect and affection for him. The story we have heard is that a tavern-keeper in his parish of Santa Cruz became enraged because the teen-agers of the community had ceased to patronise his establishment. He armed himself with a gun, called at the rectory and, on seeing Bill, shot him at point blank range five times, killing him immediately. The news spread quickly and the infuriated townspeople lynched the man that very evening. That part of Bolivia is much like the old West, with Santa Cruz as a dusty frontier town.

With Father Maddigan expected back later today, I am beginning to look forward to setting out on my own holiday in three days' time.

HOTEL CONTINENTAL, BUENOS AIRES, AUGUST 28TH.

On Sunday afternoon, August 19th, I left Monsefú and met Mike Crowley on the plane. In Lima which, incidentally, is cold and damp at this time of the year, we both received gamma globulin shots against possibilities of hepatitis and other virus hazards. We are probably both immune, but considered the precaution no waste of time. The following Wednesday we flew to Chile on a Canadian Pacific DC-8 jet. We spent a few days there with the Columban Fathers from Ireland and enjoyed exploring on foot the impressive capital city of Santiago, noting the European atmosphere and the absence of the Indian features which characterise the people of Peru who are, for the most part, either pure Indian or Spanish-Indian.

The day after our arrival we went with an Australian priest to a ski resort, several hours' drive into the mountains and, the following day, made an excursion down to San Antonio on the coast, where the Columbans and the Holy Cross Fathers both have parishes. We visited slums, but were impressed by the high attendance in the schools, the number of community libraries and the high regard for learning we found everywhere. A large proportion of the clergy of the country come from outside, but the Chilean priests have excellent training and are intellectual leaders. The students in the seminaries are, for the most part, graduates of one or other of the two very good universities in Santiago. The new cardinal, we learned, is the most influential leader in the country, but the clergy as a whole who come from the professional and wealthy classes, find themselves out of touch with the workers.

Politically, the country is not healthy; inflation, a strong, legitimate Communist party, allied with doctrinaire socialists, combine to delay the reform and consolidation of the opposing democratic parties. It makes for a dangerous situation. It is a curious fact that in the last election in 1960 the Communist front would have come to power by popular vote if it had not been for the vote-splitting brought about by an unfrocked priest who had formed his own left-wing political party. It would have been the only case, outside of Kerala in India, where the Party had won a free election. Before the next election it is hoped that the redistribution of large land-holdings and the unification of democratic parties will forestall a Communist victory.

Chileans are proud people. They dress well even when poor. Although the country is suffering from inflation now, it is much better off than Peru, as it can manufacture many of its own needed goods.

We flew from Santiago de Chile to Buenos Aires on the very same jetliner that had brought us from Lima a few days earlier. Since our arrival we have spent an afternoon with two Columban priests who look after a sailors' hostel, the Apostolate of the Sea, and an evening with the same pair, plus some Irish Pallotine priests of second generation Argentinian families and Dr. McGarry, Maynooth professor, editor of a pastoral magazine and a good friend of Mike's. In such company and in our interchanges with the Columbans we found ourselves pontificating on social problems, the quality of various bishops and other high officials as if we were in one of the smoke-filled rooms of the Vatican Council. All very enjoyable!

Mike is impressed, as am I, by the numbers of second and third generation Irish here whose voice inflection can be pin-pointed to the very county in Ireland where their forebears belonged. It is just as if they had only left that country a year ago. That is, of course, when they speak English. They spit out their Spanish like the true Argentinians they are.

The political situation here is unhappy, as in most Latin-American countries today. We find the people talk readily to strangers — which cannot be said of Peruvians. A taxi-driver confided to us that, with soldiers mixing in politics and a military junta in power, he wished he could belong to any other country in the world but his own. Still, even though civil servants and many others have remained unpaid for months, the impression we had, coming from Peru, was one of prosperity.

Buenos Aires reminded me of Montreal, except that it is bigger and more beautiful. The city abounds in parks and open spaces where tremendous crowds gather to witness sporting events such as soccer and *pato* which is somewhat like polo. Besides spectator sports, great emphasis is placed on participating sports, as evidenced by the facilities provided everywhere throughout the city.

The weather here is fair and cool and although it is not yet spring in this part of the world, there are flowers everywhere. We had a day's outing on the Tigre river which is a branch of the Parana and enjoyed the conversation of our excursion guide who is a born philosopher and a shrewd judge of the social situation in Argentina, quite as much as the lovely scenery. We noted with surprise that although

77

it was cold enough for one to see one's breath, oranges were growing on the shade-trees along the side streets within sight of the city.

On Sunday we offered Mass at the Convent of the Sisters of Mercy whose foundation goes back to the very early days here and again were astonished to hear English spoken with a delightful Irish brogue. When we met the Irish Chargé d'Affaires later it was no surprise to us to learn that immigration to this country from Ireland in the last century had been very heavy. By the time we got around to looking up the Brazilian Consul General to have our visas signed for the flight to Rio, it seemed quite natural that his name should be Dan Corbett. Our call on him led to the most interesting part of our trip. As he signed the visas he casually suggested that we get in touch with his father in Rio on our arrival. To show that he meant it, he gave us his father's telephone number.

There is a mail strike on in this city because postal workers have been left unpaid for months. I think some of the letters I have written may have been lost in a batch of mail that was destroyed, so I'll hold this over and will mail it in Brazil tomorrow.

SEPTEMBER 4TH NOW, AND SAO PAOLO, BRAZIL.

We went straight through to Rio in pursuit of Mike's friend, Dr. McGarry, whose company we had enjoyed so much in Buenos Aires. I was anxious to find him again to probe some of the ideas and data he had collected on a wisely planned and well organized tour of all South America. We had difficulty in locating him and finally gave up the search, only to meet him later, by accident, at the home of Dan Corbett, Sr.

The warmth of the welcome we received from the Corbetts made us feel as if we had always been old friends of theirs. Dan, like Mike Crowley, is a Cork man. He came to South America in his youth as an employee of a cable company, married a Belgian girl whose parents had settled in

Rio, and eventually became the successful head of a cosmetics business. In spite of the fact that he is still an ardent Irishman, none of his children speaks English perfectly. Early in their married life the parents decided to bring up their family speaking Portuguese, so as not to divide them from their countrymen. The diplomatic service seems to have an attraction for the junior Corbetts. Besides the Consul-General in Buenos Aires, another son is economic adviser to the Brazilian embassy in Warsaw.

We learned much while we were with the Corbetts. On Saturday Dan took us inland to Sao Sebastiao to visit his priest son, Peter, in his parish there. It was a six-hour trip by bus and jeep, but with Dan as our guide it was a pleasurable journey.

Peter had joined the Jesuit Order and had spent years at Fordham University in New York, but during the long retreat before last vows are taken, he decided he wanted to be a diocesan priest and withdrew from the Order. He has really found himself in parish work and is a model beyond imitation in pastoral zeal and intelligent leadership of his people. He has taken on an extensive territory which for twenty years was without a pastor. Although he is alone and has twelve or more communities to look after, he has brought each one to life and has organized things better than I would have thought possible in any rural area. Being a native is a help, but he has many assets, and coming from a wonderful family is no small part of it. For the most part but with some notable exceptions, the native clergy in Latin American countries are conservative and tradition-bound. Perhaps after the deliberations of the Ecumenical Council the Church will not look so old and out-dated as it does in those young countries today.

We were interested to hear from the Corbetts something of the work of Don Helder Camara, Coadjutor Archbishop of Rio, and the slum clearance projects he has undertaken in close co-operation with the laity. These include four blocks of apartments, each containing eight hundred units, built on a luxury beach, where only nominal rent is paid and where home management is of prime importance. Monthly prizes are offered to stimulate interest and competition in this field. He has also organized a vast market-place outside the city of Rio where farmers bring their produce which is then taken by fleets of trucks to the city market where it can be sold at profitable prices. He has devised other unusual but effective ways also to offset the consequences of economic injustice and disorganization.

Involvement in politics in Brazil can be interesting and dangerous. The Communists have allied themselves with the corrupt government of Goulart and his brother-in-law, Leonard Brizzola; there is immense, illegal import of arms through the port of Recife, within reach of Cuba, and in some provinces control of power is in the hands of bandits. Although the times are crucial, with a political situation building up that may result in anything — from a military coup to full civil war — before the election date, October 4th, Brazil continues to be one of the fastest-growing industrial areas in the world. We were impressed by the modern-age look of Rio de Janeiro which is in marked contrast to anything that can be seen in Peru.

We came on to Sao Paolo from Rio yesterday, having enjoyed every moment of our stay in that hospitable city and particularly the time we spent with the Corbett family than whom there are none finer in all South America.

Mike Crowley and Dan Corbett Senior come from different parts of County Cork in Ireland, but Mallow people and Clonakilty folk have enough mutual knowledge to talk for days, and that is how it was. I'm all listened out on subjects small and large. I was adopted as a countryman without formality. Now I must stop. The typewriter is getting tired and I have things to do before we leave for home tomorrow.

LIMA, SEPTEMBER 7TH.

We came in yesterday afternoon over the Andes from Sao Paolo, and tomorrow I'll be back in Monsefú. A more detailed record of our trip has been set down in Mike

Crowley's diary, a five-year one, given him by a parishioner in Cork whose baby was born in his Volkswagen on the way to hospital. It was begun on his arrival in Lima last year, the day before he came up with me to Monsefú.

We returned to find a growing feeling of popular approval for the Peruvian *Junta Militar* which arbitrarily took control of the government in July. They are coming to be regarded as an honest group of officers of a well-disciplined armed service who are convinced they are doing the right thing in taking over the higher and autonomous branches of government. This country needs honest administration even more urgently than the countries we have just been visiting as there is no extra wealth to waste. 'All the gold in Peru' is a phrase nostalgically reminiscent of a time when an Inca emperor's ransom could be thought of in terms of a room, seventeen feet by twenty-two, filled solidly with gold to a line drawn as high as a man's hand could reach.

MONSEFU. FEAST OF ST. FRANCIS SOLANO, 1962.

Father Ovile Meunier, O.M.I., parish priest of Chincha Alta, down the coast from Lima, spent a couple of days with us recently. He came to Peru at the age of fifty from an Oblate parish in Vancouver, B. C. and, after working for some years with the people here, told us he has no wish to be recalled to the home base. A man of great kindness and experience, he made us see facets of the Peruvian temperament and personality that were not fully realised or appreciated by us before. The Canadian Oblates, both in Chincha Alta and in their other parishes in Peru, Bolivia and Chile, have been remarkably successful. With the arrogance of youth we suggested that perhaps there was more to start with on the coast south of Lima. St. Francis Solano and a succession of zealous missionaries in other centuries had evangelized the people; they knew what their faith meant and frequented the sacraments, whereas our northern coastal people are incredibly ignorant about their faith. "You'll see, you'll see," said Father Meunier, "They'll respond won-

81

derfully." And, impatiently wanting it to be so, we believe him.

There was a tragic accident in Santa Rosa since last writing. One Sunday morning recently two brothers tried to take apart a naval shell they had found on the beach and they with their sister were killed in the ensuing explosion. It was of a type that had not been in use for over thirty years but, buried in the dry sand of the Santa Rosa beach, had remained 'live'. The father of the three is a *brujo* or medicine-man of the pre-Christian school. None of the family has ever learned to read or write, although that impediment does not prevent a *brujo* from making a better living than a qualified doctor in these parts.

The year is nearing an end and, for us, it is a time of change. The new parish of Cayalti-Zana is now fully organized. For some months past, Father Bill Cooney has been going there on his own, looking after the many thousands in the hacienda and in the town of Zana, returning to the presbytery here for a meal only once in two days. He is now established in a temporary presbytery in Cayalti, and Father Paul Mooney has gone to join him.

Zana, the seat of the parish, is where St. Toribio, second archbishop of Lima, died on his way back from an arduous pastoral journey. It was once the third city of Peru, less in importance only than Lima and Trujillo, but it is almost a ghost town today. Henry Morgan and other pirates sacked it in raids many times in the days of its glory and in the eighteenth century it was damaged almost to destruction by a great flood. The ruins of many magnificent churches are still to be seen there as well as the remains of many of the earlier Indian settlements. It was under interdict for more than two centuries, due to some curious lapse of ecclesiastical memory. Only a few years ago, when the Bishop of Chiclayo discovered that the ancient interdict had never been lifted, was the situation remedied.

The people of Zana are a mixture of Negro, Indian and Spanish. They live in great poverty yet are by nature friendly and happy. They have the reputation of being very good cooks, and a candy they make is famous throughout Peru. The town has a population of about three thousand while Cayalti, the hacienda or commercial farm-factory nearby, has twenty thousand. There is a fine modern church in Zana, built by German priests who were there some years ago but who have since left. The town has nothing else but ruins of its past greatness.

Cayalti is the hacienda visited by Prince Philip when he was in Chiclayo last year. It has always had bonds with Monsefú. Every day two truckloads of labourers go from here to work in the sugar-cane fields there for seventy to eighty cents a day, which is not enough to take care of even the minimal needs of a family. In the hacienda system which is the dominant form of land tenure in Peru, human dignity has no place. Even the best of administrators of these huge organizations often satisfy their obligations to society by giving charity without justice while the worst sometimes give piety without either.

Father Jim Doody has completed his language studies in Lima and will return with me to Monsefú next week when I go south to attend to some business and, perhaps, if time permits, to pay a visit to the Pucallpa jungle region where the Montreal Pont Viau Mission Society is working.

The Convent is nearing completion and it is hoped that the Sisters will be able to move into it before the end of the year.

Television is coming to Chiclayo. Everything has been ready for the past six months, but there hasn't been enough electric power. Now, I suspect, the power will be supplied by cutting the amount available to Monsefú and other outside communities, as two nights ago the lights went out again, leaving us once more on candle-power.

The Ursuline Sisters from Ontario have arrived to open
the school in Chiclayo that has been such a source of soul-
searching for us all. The two youngest remained in Lima
while the Mother Superior and the future Principal of the
school came on here — only to find that the house that had
been promised them is not available and the committee
which had been sponsoring the school had disbanded. They
are now seeking another house in town. They are determined
to go ahead with the idea if it is feasible at all, because
those were the instructions given them by their Mother
General and by Bishop Cody. The London priests would
like them to drop the whole idea and come to help them.
However, the St. Joseph Sisters are on their way now to do
just that.

As I write I am listening to Porfirio, age ten, who helps
Petita in the kitchen when he is not in the Sisters' school.
He is singing in his high, boy's voice the latest blasting
Afro-Latin song on the Monsefú hit parade, 'A la Vincenta
Yo me Voy'; and at my feet, lying on its back after sipping
the hemlock 'Real-Kill' which I just sprayed on the window,
lies a big fly, buzzing an accompaniment.

Monsefu, December 8, 1962.

The elderly gentleman who came to the Presbytery as
to a last refuge, did not look like a man from the mountains.
He was dressed elegantly, sporting both tie and waistcoat.
Nevertheless, this Don Rafael was more at home on a horse
in the hills than he was sitting spider-like at his desk in a
Chiclayo office. His brother, he told us, owned a hacienda
in Silugan, a small place far up in the high sierra. The people were anxious to have a priest come for the annual feast,
as the pastor of their parish of Querecotillo was sick in hospital and had not been among them for six months. They
had sought elsewhere, but no one was free to go at that
particular time. Don Rafael diffidently mentioned his two

nephews who are seminarians, and that disposed us to do what we could for him. Two seminarians in a family is a very seldom thing in Peru.

Bishop Figueroa was much in favour of the undertaking and was prepared to give missionary faculties to any priest who would agree to go. John Maddigan, I felt, was the one who was most in need of a holiday. He hadn't slept for the past three nights because of noisy celebrations in the square outside the presbytery and the blare of band instruments, emphasized by loud-speakers, which kept up until near dawn. The mountains, I thought, would be peaceful. He would get a chance of a rest. And it would do Jim Doody good to go too, as he had only recently come to Monsefú after several months of concentrated language study in Lima.

So, on Tuesday, November 27th, the two priests drove off in the Volkswagen, laden with all their needs for Mass as well as personal accoutrements, sun helmets against the tropical day, light wind-breakers against the evening chill of the mountains, and a supply of bully-beef as an insurance against hunger. They called for Don Rafael in Chiclayo and, in the next seven hours zig-zagged high into the mountains, until at last the going became impossible, the road ended at a river and the car had to be abandoned — much to the relief of Don Rafael who kept getting car-sick at intervals.

It was late afternoon when they came to the end of the road. Don Rafael was in favour of remaining overnight by the side of the river which they would have to ford, but a glance into the squalid cane huts which provided the only shelter made the priests decide to press right on to Silugan. Don Rafael, feeling that luck must always be with a priest, bit his moustache nervously and agreed. Half an hour later, aided by a cable and pulleys, they found themselves on the other side of the river where mules, already strapped up and ready to go, were waiting for them.

Don Rafael did not venture to tell the priests that there was a seven-hour journey ahead of them, nor did he draw attention to the fact that the trail had never before been travelled at night, nor even hint that one mis-step by man or beast could carry a traveller down a thousand feet or more. The trail crawled along the spine of the Great Divide which separates the waters that flow to the Atlantic from those that flow to the Pacific.

Mules are sure-footed creatures, even in the dark. The priests, when they saw by daylight, on the return journey, the trail that threads its way through the clouds, were filled with amazement, and developed a confidence in their mounts they had scarcely felt that night. Father Jim had some previous acquaintance with the genus 'horse', but Father John scarcely knew mane from tail. What horse sense he possesses, he says, comes from Roy Rogers. Somehow, they managed to mount the beasts and jogged along bravely, with Father Jim singing 'The Brave Fenian Men' and Father John 'The Donkey Serenade', or so he says.

Two young boys had been sent from Silugan to act as guides over the dangerous trail. They were barefoot and seemed to give no thought to the sharp rocks. Father John felt so sorry for them that he made up his mind to dismount after an hour or two and let them take turns riding for a while. His resolution came to nothing, however, for after two hours in the saddle he was too stiff and sore to dismount without assistance. As for walking, he doubted if his legs would bear the weight of his body.

As the little group moved slowly along the trail and the mules twisted around the curves and their forefeet dropped into the darkness, Don Rafael, who had fully recovered and was now in his own element, amused himself by calling out every few minutes, "Beep-beep! Look out for the car!" By the time five hours had passed with agonizing slowness, the joke was wearing as thin as some portions of gringo hide. Father Jim, as he listened to the river waters rushing in the depths below, began to wonder how far was down. Father John became concerned about a pain that developed in the back of his neck, until he discovered the cause of it — he was grinding his teeth, hard.

The sure-footed mules kept on going, showing no fear of the trail and no pity for the riders. Shortly after eleven o'clock Silugan was in sight, and the mountains rang with shouts that the priests were coming. Father Jim greeted all he could see and many whom he could not, and Father John resumed singing the Donkey Serenade. The boys guiding his mule kept shouting something that sounded like a sneeze and each time he politely wished them 'Salud!' — until they took to yelling 'Mule!' at the animals instead.

It was midnight when they finally reached Silugan and the joy of arriving was marred only by the fact that a welcoming rocket caused the lead mule to panic, and Father John was thrown clean off into the bush. He was badly scratched, but otherwise suffered no damage, and was consoled by the fact that he was finally down from that tonnage of torture.

The band played its welcoming numbers under the night sky. The missioners stood — they could do nothing else for the first few minutes — and waited until the addresses of welcome were read by the light of torches. When the formalities were over they asked to be shown to their room where, after a prayer of fervent thankfulness for their safe arrival, they prepared for bed and drifted off into a sound slumber, pausing only to consider how fortunate the world was that Henry Ford was ever born.

The next morning the village chapel was crowded to the doors with people seeking to go to confession, to be married, to have their babies baptised. Lines were formed and an effort was made to create order out of chaos. Father John stood before a row of twenty babies, big and angry enough to swing punches, and tried to be heard above the protests of the infants as he administered the sacrament of baptism to each in turn. A couple of feet behind the row of babies and their sponsors, Father Doody was attempting to perform the marriage service for a half-dozen couples, trying in his newly acquired foreign tongue, to be heard above both the infants and his confrère. And all the while, both priests were being shouted down with requests for blessings of various objects. This last appeared to take precedence over the sacraments in the minds of most of the people. In the midst of all this confusion a schoolmaster from the village of La Capilla, two and a half hour's ride away by muleback, pleaded with the missioners to include his village in their schedule. He had over two hundred pupils ready for confession, he said.

The following morning at daybreak, over a meal of hard-boiled eggs, Father John and Father Jim agreed that the excursion to La Capilla could be fitted into their holiday plans. That afternoon at about 4 o'clock, when most of the work they had come to Silugan to do had been attended to, they set out.

As they entered La Capilla on their mules they were welcomed by a march-past of two hundred school-children and, of course, another brass band. After they had been brought to the room off the sacristy which was to be their sleeping quarters they were conducted to a nearby dwelling for a meal. This was a very formal affair, presided over by the local officials. Foods they had never encountered before were put before them and eaten, but not with much enthusiasm. When the speeches and other formalities were over, the priests went to the chapel where they heard two hundred and fifty confessions, baptized fifteen babies brought by their sponsors in groups of two to five, convalidated a dozen marriages and, at midnight, led a procession around the square in front of the chapel. A 1 a.m. snack of 'hermitas', a tasteless local fruit, and a glass of champagne crowned the day.

The next morning when the priests arrived at the chapel to prepare for the seven o'clock Mass, they found a line-up for baptisms and marriages. It was 9.30 before the seven o'clock Mass was begun. By 10.30 they were ready to bid *adios* to La Capilla and set out on their way back to Silugan.

Mass in Silugan, scheduled for 11.00 was postponed to 1.00 o'clock; the departure for the next mission on the list, Santa Clara, set for 2.00 o'clock, was delayed until five. From then on the priests decided not to set definite hours for any ceremonies, except to say that Masses would be offered in the forenoon. Marriages, baptisms, confessions and blessings would be from 7 a.m. until midnight, with minimum time out for meals.

It was only an hour's ride from Silugan to Santa Clara. On arriving they were surprised to see a sign on the church door in two-feet high letters, 'MARRIAGES FREE'. They had previously explained that they would not take any money from the people as the hacienda owner in Silugan had presented them with a thousand soles, or forty dollars, for the expenses of the trip. As a man's earnings only amount to ten soles a day in that mountain region, the sign and the scramble to get married are understandable.

Since Father John, encouraged by an immediate response which for him distinguished these mountain people from the self-willed people on the coast, found that he had become very fluent in giving instructions in Spanish, Father Jim left him to look after the marriage situation and went himself on a sick call several hours' distant by mule-back, where an old patriarch lay dying. People like this old man had, for generations, kept the faith alive in these parts, in spite of the fact that visits from priests were rare events.

It was good luck for the visitors that it had not rained for the first four days of the mission. When, on the fifth day the rains came in Santa Clara, the mud was so slippery that Father Jim claimed that it took two men to hold one man up.

As time began to run out, the pleas for blessings intensified. Of all strange objects brought for this purpose, the most curious was a painted human skull which was said to have belonged to a man who had been killed in an accident. The present owner of this gruesome object is a *brujo* or witch-doctor. Needless to say, his request was refused.

When, at last, the priests were able to wrench themselves free, they returned to Silugan to sleep. They were awakened at dawn by the sound of chickens, clucking and scratching, and it was some time before they realised they were under the beds. After their usual breakfast of boiled eggs which contributed towards a total count of seventy-two consumed by them in six days, they went back to their room where Father John found a thank-offering laid on his bed by a grateful hen.

On Monday morning, after saying Mass in Silugan, the priests prepared for the long journey back by mule and Volkswagen. It was not enough to wave a cheery good-bye. They had to give a firm promise to return and to swing half-down from their mounts to be embraced by people who would have given much to keep them there. Don Rafael, who had wept quietly when Father John preached on matrimony, said he intended to get his own marriage blessed soon. More than a hundred pounds of coffee beans were slung across the mules as gifts for the bishop and for the priests themselves.

The results of the mission into the high sierra are known only to God, but statistics would indicate that it was a successful effort and were certainly encouraging for the priests. The record, over a period of six days, showed that seventy baptisms, and thirty marriages had been performed and over six hundred confessions had been heard. And the missioners had logged twenty-five hours of mule-back travel.

It was near midnight on December 3rd. when Father Jim and Father John walked into the presbytery in Monsefú, all set after their holiday to tackle the duties that were lined up for the next three days — one thousand children's confessions and five hundred and sixty confirmations. They had had the time of their lives, they insisted, and Father John had lost the cold he had taken with him into the hills. Who would deny that a change is as good as a rest?

MONSEFU, DECEMBER 28, 1962

News that Reverend Mother Assumpta, Mother General of the Mercy Sisters in Newfoundland, and Mother Imelda who formerly held that post, were coming on an official visit to their newest foundation and that they would remain to spend Christmas with the Sisters, made us stop and think. The cramped quarters of Dr. Custodio's house could not be expanded to house the visitors and, with the long vacation coming up, there would be no problem about our being given space again in the school. So we have moved out and turned our new presbytery over to the Sisters. They had at no time complained about their discomforts, and until schools closed at the end of the year we could not have done anything about the situation anyway. But now this solution is happy for us all. We are keeping the office section of the presbytery for our own use and are living like kings on the good meals the Sisters prepare for us. The fact that I counted forty termites in bed with me on my first night in the school is a minor incidental discomfort that weighs lightly against the Sisters' good cooking.

Reverend Mother Assumpta and Mother Imelda arrived on the day of prize-giving in the government schools and were put to work at once, giving out prizes and diplomas. They made a profound impression in their white habits, complete with white gloves which added to the formality of their attire. The quality of soul and their interest in the people did not need language to be expressed. During their stay, when they were not being thumped on the back in enthusiastic greeting or were not busy with the other Sisters in taking part in their daily activities, they found quiet corners for contemplation or walked in the presbytery grounds saying more prayers than their busy lives at home would ever have given them time for.

One of the greatest joys of their visit was the concert given by our parish school. A hundred and twenty children, from five to eight years of age, of a different race and language, had been awakened and developed so much in just one year that it was hard to believe this miracle had really happened, even though we were there to see it.

The children's concert was so good that it was given again in Chiclayo, this time with the director of a television station present. The result was that on Christmas Eve many of the children performed on television in song and dance and with a rhythm band. Chiclayo is still talking about the transformation of the Indians of Monsefú into cultured little ladies and gentlemen. The manager of the Power Company in Chiclayo said it was a great pity that all this good education was being wasted on the *cholos* of Monsefú. "Educate a *cholo*," he said, "and you educate another thief!" Then, as an afterthought, he added, "or a revolutionary." It is our hope that these small people will eventually revolutionise things in their native Monsefú, but not in the way that was meant. It is our further hope that all Peru will

91

benefit by what is being done for its young people by the good schools that are being given them by North American Sisters working in co-operation with priest teams all through their land.

The Priest's Man has just come in to tell me that the donkey will be at the side door at 5.30, and will I please tell Father Maddigan. The message is one to ponder over. Today is Sister Mary Dorothy's feast day, and I'm thinking Fathers Jim and John are maybe planning a little surprise for the Mother Superior of the Mercy Sisters. I am thinking, too, that before sundown we may have a donkey in our house.

One of the quaint customs of our little corner of the world is the sharing of the homes with the little brothers of St. Francis. There is scarcely a house in the parish that does not bear resemblance to a Noah's ark inside. A horse or a donkey may sometimes be seen wandering, apparently aimlessly, down the street, but if one's attention is diverted, even momentarily, the animal suddenly becomes invisible. Only the flick of a tail from an open doorway betrays the fact that he has entered 'his' house; and not a donkey in town but knows his own home. The front entrance is usually the only approach to the back yard. I am hoping that Bishop Carter, when he comes later today won't think we have gone native.

The London priests, Bill Cooney and Paul Mooney, were delighted when they heard that Bishop Emmett Carter, the recently appointed auxiliary bishop of their home diocese was coming to visit them. He is with them now in Cayalti, but will be with us later today to give us a talk on Catechetics, a subject which is a special interest of his and a special concern of ours, since instruction in the faith is our only way of combatting the influences that have gradually, over the centuries, added a strong flavour of superstition to the religious practices of our people. Already we have removed the revered statue of the Captive Lord from public view, hoping that the importance of Mass and the Sacraments would be given greater emphasis if minor religious devotions were played down. No one raised any serious objection at first, but when lack of rain in the mountains and consequent near-drought in coastal areas threatened crops, murmurings were heard. A deputation of farmers called at the presbytery and pointed out that the Captive Lord had always been regarded as the protector of agriculture and that the present crisis would not have arisen if we had not discouraged the people's faith. We told them that the statue of the Captive Lord would be exposed for veneration if it would help them to pray, but that Confession and Holy Communion were a more vital means of stimulating their faith. It will be interesting to see how things will turn out.

Religious feasts throughout Bolivia and Peru have always been marked by processions through the streets with, as the years grew into centuries, more emphasis on feasting than on religion. Monsefú holds over a hundred regular religious processions a year, most of which become for the people little more than occasions of drunken celebrations.

We have cancelled permanently two of the regular processions in which the statue of the Captive Lord is carried through the streets, but not without great argument and hot debate. The Canadian parliament on a burning issue, could not have produced more flaming rhetoric.

The main feast in honour of the Captive Lord is celebrated annually on September 14th, but since a year is too long to wait, there is also a mid-year feast; and then there is the octave of the mid-year feast which, for the past ten years, has been honoured by two processions because of a dispute which occurred among the mayordomos. We pointed out that Pope John XXIII has abolished observance of octaves of feasts except for Christmas, Easter and Pentecost; that the important thing is the Holy Sacrifice of the Mass; that money collected to pay for brass bands in the processions would be better used on more lasting things, either in the church or in their own homes. And we drew attention to the fact that when the statue is brought through the streets too often no one pays very much attention. The

93

mayordomos resisted with arguments about the will of the people; the need to encourage religious fervour by processions, especially by giving the people an opportunity of venerating publicly the most beloved statue of the parish. They spoke fervently of the importance of tradition and, in a ploy, admitting the supreme value of the sacraments, pleaded for one last year of doing things the old-time way, while in sermons the people would be prepared for the changes that would come. I invoked the mental image of a certain Vicar General of an Archdiocese, well known to me and said, "The answer is No!" With that closure all rhetoric ended, but I expect the bishop in Chiclayo will be bothered with a delegation.

MONSEFU, FEBRUARY 8TH, 1963.

Bishop Carter's visit has been a great treat, to say little. Two days ago he was at the beach with us and came here to give a talk to ourselves, the Mercy Sisters and the four Ursulines from Chatham, Ontario, who are now in Chiclayo. He stayed to share a grand meal in honour of Sister Dorothy, it being her feast day, and to join in the fun of the occasion.

I was reminded of the mysterious message which had been delivered earlier that day, when there was a loud knocking at the door and two strangers presented themselves with a donkey. One of them led it in and, when it stuck momentarily in the passage, the other placed a large foot firmly on the animal's rump and shoved it into the patio. They led it over to a surprised Sister Dorothy and solemnly offered it to her as a gift in celebration of the occasion. They then asked to be presented to the eminent prelate who, they had heard, was visiting Monsefú. Bishop Carter said later that two more villainous-looking characters he had never seen. However, when the disguises were penetrated, the 'visitors' turned out to be Fathers Jim and John.

Bishop Carter's talk on new orientation in catechetics was one we will all profit from. He also showed us slides he had taken inside the Vatican Council, with a running commentary which made us see his vision of a greatly improved future as a result of it.

Not far from fifteen years ago he was telling me to "think with the Church", not with the Catholic Worker. Now he's making me feel that I'm too conservative. Maybe we've both changed.

MONSEFU, MARCH 8TH, 1963

We have had a flurry of visitors lately. One day last week Father Jerome Deagan of the St. James Society drove down from his post in Piura in Father Tom Reilly's car. He announced that Father Tom was on his way from Lima with two Canadian friends, Lucien and Dorothea Maynard. This was good news for us. Father Tom is always a welcome visitor — since the hard days of 1961 when he came to visit and stayed to help, sharing the old, windowless, termite-infested mud-brick presbytery which we called home. The Maynards, too, were not strangers to us, although we had never seen them. Through Father Tom they had become interested in our work and had sent us substantial proof of their concern for us. They turned up later on their own by bus from Lima. It was a fourteen-hour journey in sizzling equatorial heat, the discomforts of which they must have foreseen, since they had already experienced the misery of bus travel in these regions by driving to La Paz from Cochabamba over almost impassable roads and through mountain floods.

A rest in Chiclayo had restored them to cheerfulness and when they arrived in Monsefú in time for Mass they were feeling fresh and energetic. Lucien was carrying a big movie camera balanced on his arm like a tommy-gun. His wife gave him his first assignment — to 'shoot' the three bright little six-year-olds who had served Mass and whom the Sisters had trained to perfection.

To give our visitors an appetite for breakfast, they were taken to the market-place where Lucien was not quite fast enough on the trigger to get a good shot of a young woman carrying a huge bowl of shellfish on her head and a baby chewing contentedly on a piece of fish in a sling on her back; but he climbed on an unused table and shot everyone within range.

Father Tom arrived by plane in mid-morning and the same plane took two other visitors of ours, Fathers Don Ballou and John Auer, north to Talara. Shortly afterwards Father Butler, a Columban priest from Liverpool, England, who works in the new slums in Lima, but who had come north for a brief holiday, dropped in to salute us. And there were Vincentians from Chiclayo and a Redemptorist from Piura who came to tell us that Sisters from his parish were planning to visit our Mercy Sisters that morning. On that same day Father Tex Mitchell arrived in pursuit of Fathers Ballou and Auer and that night shared our quarters in the school.

The Maynards would have stayed longer but for the news of the impending general election in Canada which had reached them in Panama on their way down. As Lucien is a candidate for the Social Credit Party in Alberta he felt he had to return quickly to do some campaigning.

The same week brought us two Californian doctors from the hospital ship 'Hope' which has recently finished a year's mercy mission on the coast of Peru. They bought woven straw souvenirs to bring home and offered us the facilities of their hotel in Chiclayo if we felt the need of a hot shower or a cold drink.

Now, with Visitors' Week behind us, things have returned to normal.

The blessing of the Mercy Sisters' new convent was a very happy occasion. The Auxiliary Bishop of Chiclayo, Bishop Sanchez-Moreno, came at 9 a.m. on Monday, February 25th, to bless the new building and celebrate the first Mass in the chapel. The people are well used to blessings — I was asked to bless a slaughter-house only yesterday — but they regard such occasions as purely social ones, with the *padrinos* of whatever is blessed bringing handsome gifts. Everyone, of course, enjoys the consequent toasting.

96

This was the first occasion in Monsefú when Mass accompanied the blessing.

That very afternoon the move was on, with beds and baggage being carted into the new convent in such swift order that the Sisters were able to sleep there that night. They made no complaint about the fact that the only available truck for transporting their gear was one that is normally used for carrying sugar-cane. After a day or two spent in getting settled the Sisters left for Lima where they will go on Retreat before taking a week's holiday. When they return, four Sisters of St. Joseph will share their convent for a few weeks before going to Cayalti to see what they can do with the ten thousand children waiting for them in the London priests' new parish.

With the Sisters at last happily established in their beautiful new convent, we lost no time in occupying our presbytery again. This time we knew we were in permanent possession.

MONSEFU, MARCH 15TH.

Each day brings us a little closer to an understanding of our people. That the devil still walks abroad, we have ample proof. The old-established profession of the *brujo* (pronounced broo-ho) or witch-doctor still flourishes. Its headquarters and seat of learning are in nearby Salas, where there are so many *brujos* that it is said they cannot move without bumping into one another. Even this small town boasts several who are well-known, besides a number of semi-professionals. They are among the most prosperous of our citizens. Indeed we have found to our astonishment, that a *brujo* commands higher fees than a genuine medical man.

Some are only 'healers' who diagnose an illness by moving a guinea-pig over the body of the patient and observing the reactions of the little animal; their treatment consists of 'cleaning' the person with stones and giving drinks made from jungle herbs or perhaps even recognized drugs obtained from a pharmacy. The methods of the real *brujos* are more elaborate. They go off into the lonely places in the early hours of the morning and 'set a table', as they say. By means of potions they put themselves — or sometimes the sick person — in a trance and, with much shaking of rattles and shouting of gibberish, call on the spirits to intervene. Often they use images of saints in a sacrilegious attempt to give their superstitious practices the appearance of being sanctioned by the Church. Besides undertaking to cure an illness they will often indicate its cause, usually the jealousy of some person whom they name. Sometimes they will administer 'justice' at a price by sending a medicine to afflict with weakness or even kill the suspected third party.

One of the most powerful figures in Monsefú is one Tomas Tullume. For the last six months he has been banned from being god-father in baptisms and marriages because of his sinister reputation. Where ignorance flourishes, the *brujos* grow wealthy. When it begins to diminish as a result of more and better schooling and more religious instruction, Tomas Tullume and his kind will be forced to give up their nefarious trade.

If I were asked to give proof of the devil's influence in the affairs of men, I would not point to cases of demoniac possession, nor even to the activities of the *brujos*, but I would point to the chaos that exists in every area of human life, particularly in family life. Every morning when we return from parish visiting we bring home painful stories of domestic problems. Almost half our parishioners are involved in illicit unions, though most of them see nothing wrong in such a situation. They say they did not have time to prepare; or they had no money for the wedding feast; or they had parents who were in mourning and so could not plan a wedding celebration; or perhaps parents who were not happy about the marriage. Even among those who are legally married, few have had any religious instruction and the majority see nothing wrong in adultery if things go badly at home. On the brighter side, our people have a great love for children and there are few offspring of illicit unions who are not recognized by their fathers and cherished by them.

While on the subject of manifestations of diabolic influence, I should not omit mention of the inescapable noises that plague us here. Hell must surely be the source of the disturbance we suffer from, night after night, when dances go on until near dawn in the centre of town, quite close to our presbytery. They are accompanied always by the same five tunes in the same one rhythm which are broadcast, along with a continuous whistle from the amplifier, over a powerful loud-speaker system. Sometimes the movie theatre picks up the bombastic advertisements of a Chiclayo radio station and amplifies them all over town until you can't hear your own teeth grinding. There are occasions, too, when the celebration of the Feast of the day goes on through the night as well, with exuberant barrages of rocketry. At least the Sisters are away from all that in their new convent on the edge of the town.

Noise at funerals is customary also and brings to mind Our Lord's admonition to the mourners at the beside of the daughter of Jairus. In Monsefú, instead of offering prayers for the person who has just died, members of the family generally burst into wailing complaints to the departed soul, "Aye, little brother, why do you go and leave me here all alone?" "Aye, little mother of my heart, why are you doing this to us. Why do you wish to leave us orphans?" The wailing comes in a two-tone chant, each one on his own, and when more than five compete for control of the floor the din grows so loud that thinking becomes impossible. It is astonishing to observe how a person in the grip of built-up hysteria, with tears flowing generously, will stop suddenly when he is told sharply that THIS IS NOT THE TIME for that sort of thing. It seems cruel to put a stop to their expressions of anguish, but they don't really seem to mind being rescued from a painful custom which demands hysterics and cheapens real grief.

99

The end of March brings the end of summer to Monsefú and with April and cooler weather the children return to school. This year the Sisters' school is probably the only one in the whole country to open on time. The Ministry of Education has postponed the return to classes in the government schools because of problems which have not been publicly spelled out, although indications are that a teachers' strike is imminent. Other private schools remain closed because the pupils have not turned up for classes. Here in the parish the picture is very different. Parents and children are all impatient for school to open. The Sisters, happy to be living at last in a convent of their own which is far removed from the noise and tumult of the centre of town, are eager to get back to work.

The chapel-hall adjoining the church where the statue of the Captive Lord is kept and which was divided by partitions to form three class-rooms, is no longer large enough to contain the classes. We have cleaned out a store-room off the sanctuary in the church and made it into a fourth class-room. Where we go from there I do not dare to guess. At least we can manage for the coming year.

The four Sisters of St. Joseph who returned with our Sisters from Lima are still with us as their quarters in Cayalti are not yet ready. There is a very happy relationship among the members of the 'amalgamated' Order, and the 'rules' that have been light-heartedly laid down by us and as light-heartedly adopted by them include one that forbids the Mercy Sisters from using the exclamation 'Joseph!' in moments of frustration and the St. Joseph Sisters from expressing astonishment with 'Mercy me!'

Our second parish census has almost been completed and, although we have not done as well as we had hoped in fixing up irregularities in family life, we have certainly come to know the people better and, as a result, are much better able to look after them. For one thing, we find that there is no more effective way of learning the kind of Spanish that is spoken here than by talking with the people in their own homes. As in the outports in Newfoundland many a phrase is commonly used that belongs to an English of an earlier century, so here with Spanish. The people do not use many 'dictionary' words and for new-comers like Father Doody that makes listening more instructive than studying. For that matter, there are times when we all wish for greater fluency in getting a message home to our parishioners. It is not only a language barrier that separates us from them. We have become aware that we are trying to talk across the centuries to a primitive people who have a cult of virility and a racial memory of polygamy and who live under a social system that is slowly dying. There is a natural goodness in these people. We have evidence of that in the ready response we get from the children who are our hope for the future. At the same time, we know that there can be no lasting good unless we can lift the parents out of their stagnation and put family life on a sound and secure footing.

We have our good moments when we are cheered to see that many of our people are making big efforts to co-operate, but we have other moments too, when we feel like the frog who was trying to get out of the well and who found that every leap upward brought him sliding farther back down the wall. A man came to see me today who was baptized last week at the age of thirty-four, together with his four children. He was to come back the next morning to be married, but today he tells me that his bride has rheumatism and they will have to postpone the marriage for a while. We both know that this is a lie, but nothing I could say could make him aware of the importance either of the sacrament itself or of regularising his family life.

I have lived among the *cholos* of Peru now for long enough to feel a deep concern for their good and for the good of their country and I share with the best of Peruvians a burning anger against the social injustices which impede that good. I am firmly convinced that the future of this country can be great. The present social and economic system cannot last indefinitely against the forces that are even now moving relentlessly forward. But it will take much hard work and patient understanding to bring a sense of human dignity and an awareness of human responsibility into the lives of a people who have lived for too many generations in a state of economic misery.

The drop of a few degrees in temperature which heralds our tropic winter, the slight marshalling of sand into little ridges under cool breezes and the occasional cloudiness in the sky which tempers the heat of the sun all tend to give us undisputed possession of the Santa Rosa beach at this time of year. To prove that our missionary lot is not without material consolations, I took a picture today of Father Jim Doody standing on the beach near the wrecked ship which is our land-mark. If it were not for the sun helmet and cigar he would easily pass for the fellow that stands perennially outside Cash's tobacco store in St. John's, advertising 'Mayo's Cut Plug'.

We have recent news from Canada that Archbishop Skinner will visit us before the end of this month. There will be big doings in the town when this is known and I expect he will meet with an enthusiastic welcome. We ourselves are glad he will have an opportunity of seeing what has been accomplished in the three years since his last visit here. At that time he was not allowed inside the church as the key was still in the possession of the excommuniqués.

MONSEFU, MAY, 1963

The visit of Archbishop Skinner and Monsignor Summers will long be remembered by the people of Monsefú. As I had thought, the news of their coming created great interest and excitement and on their arrival a wave of enthusiasm which almost engulfed them swept through the town. The fathers of the school children, even though they were unaware of the surprise that was to come to them in the promise of a new school building, arranged a reception that I am sure would have impressed the president of the United States.

Going direct from the airport in Chiclayo, His Grace called on Bishop Figueroa at his residence. There, he found,

102

a cavalcade had formed to conduct him to Monsefú, ten miles away. At the entrance to our town he was invited to mount a flower-decked truck which jolted at a snail's pace towards the church behind a thousand or more school-children and members of religious sodalities, ducking under strings of paper pennants in papal and Peruvian colours and through bamboo arches decorated with fruit and flowers. Monsignor Summers was safe enough, seated in the rear, but His Grace was pelted with rice and nearly buried in flowers. Two bands joined the procession. Their harmony was punctuated at every half-bar by soaring rockets. After a triumphal turn around the central square, His Grace celebrated Mass. He told the people of his happiness in being again in Monsefú, this time in the company of his priests and the Mercy Sisters from his archdiocese. Father Masciarelli, Superior of the St. James Society priests in Peru, assisted in the sanctuary as he had done on the day we took over the parish. Children of the Sisters' school sang the Mass in Spanish and many of their parents received Holy Communion.

From there on there was no end to the enthusiasm of the welcome. The people could hardly believe that high dignitaries of the Church would be willing to remain for two whole weeks in the surroundings of their undistinguished little town, denying themselves all tourist attractions. But they made it clear that they had come to be with us and with the people of Monsefú and had no intention of moving far afield. Only one day was given to the capital city of Lima on their way north and a few hours on their way back, with a visit to the Apostolic Nuncio on both occasions. Except for a quick pilgrimage to the shrines of St. Martin de Porres and of St. Rose, the fascinating capital of Peru received scant attention from them.

On the two Sundays they were with us the Archbishop and Monsignor Summers celebrated Mass in our church in Monsefú and also in the mission chapels of Santa Rosa and Callanca. In Valle Hermosa where Mass is offered only a few times during the year, they visited the school and were presented with gifts of flowers, vegetables and eggs, shyly offered by people who had never before seen anyone of such eminence near their homes.

Some of the addresses read to the visitors in the course of their stay were interesting. In the fishing settlement of Santa Rosa where we have always found the people hard-bitten and apathetic in their attitude towards the church, the mayor led the schoolchildren in parade to the Mass. At the door of the chapel he gave a speech of welcome, closing with the request "that Your Grace pray to the Divine Lord that my people may continue to enjoy health and happiness, for it is with sacrifice that we launch out into the sea to seek sustenance for our children."

On the feast of St. Toribio, once Archbishop of Lima, we all attended a meeting of the clergy in Bishop Figueroa's residence in Chiclayo where His Grace was presented with a silver tray engraved with the thanks of the Chiclayo diocese. On that occasion, in welcoming Archbishop Skinner, Bishop Figueroa reminded him that on his earlier visit, almost three years ago, he had sown seed in soil that looked dry and hard and spiny, but had returned to find a spiritual garden beginning to bloom.

In the speeches that followed then and at other times during the visitors' stay, a curious assortment of names and allusions cropped up. On one occasion Archbishop Skinner and Monsignor Summers were likened to John Cabot and Jacques Cartier 'who founded a new civilization on primitive shores'. The heresy (to Newfoundland ears) that Cabot's landfall was in Cape Breton was expressed but was forgiven.

Towards the end of the visit we got the distinct impression that, to many of the people of Monsefú, Newfoundland was just another name for Canada and in the final farewell it was stated, "We send through Your Grace our respectful salutations to our Catholic brothers of the great country of Canada."

The day the visitors left town there was a greater-than-ever outburst of enthusiasm, and if the Archbishop had not been sitting in a van and sealed in by glass, he would have been buried in flowers and crushed to death in the rush for his blessing.

For us the heady after-taste of that happy visit is that next year we are to have a school building to expand into.

MONSEFU, JUNE 5TH, 1963

In the words of the old come-all-ye:

"It's only by patience and courage and grit
And eating plain food that we keeps ourselves fit."

On the whole, Newfoundlanders turned Monsefuanos are pretty hardy characters, but I am sorry to have to report that one of that hardy crew is now in sick bay. Sister Ana Maria is under medical orders to stay quiet for some time to come. She is recovering from a heart attack that must have been impending for some time although the condition only became apparent last week. She is under expert medical care through the good offices of our friend, Dr. Ricardo Ramirez-Gaston. For a few days we were all very worried about her, but the danger now seems past. Meanwhile she is being babied and spoiled by everyone — although there is little let-up in the usual teasing wherein she gives as good as she gets.

At least we have one happy item of news to report. We have just heard that three priests from the diocese of Bridgeport, Connecticut, will soon be here to work in the mountain parish of Santa Cruz which is in the Chiclayo diocese. We know something about the area because we have been helping out there during Holy Week for the past two years. It is a parish of over forty thousand people, scattered over a wide territory, most of which is without roads. In the town itself and in a number of the outlying places the Catholic faith is solid and strong — a very rare state of affairs in Peru. The people go to the sacraments at least every year and are very well aware that Mass and the sacraments are central to the faith, while devotion to statues and other private practices are peripheral. There are at least nine or ten priests serving in Peru who have come from Santa Cruz, a town of not more than four thousand in population. So it can be said that it is and will be the heartland in this country for vocations, if only its good tradition can survive the current dangerous trends. The little town is hard to reach by road, but it has an advantage in an emergency landing field which is perfectly satisfactory for the small Piper Cub plane which Father Paul Mooney now flies.

Father Paul and Father Bill Cooney are now well established in their parish of Cayalti-Zana. They are building a presbytery in Zana in order to be independent of the giant Hacienda Cayalti, the factory-farm which controls the economy of the district. The Sisters of St. Joseph have completed their first month of residence in Cayalti where they are giving religious instruction to many thousands of children.

To complete the bulletin on clerical activities, Father Rudy Masciarelli has been replaced by Father John Thomas as Superior of the St. James Society in Peru. Both have been good friends of ours from the beginning and we are happy that Father Rudy will not be far away, as he is taking over the nearby parish of Piura.

Peru is holding elections this week, and I hope the results will be known soon after the ballots are in. It was a matter of several weeks last year and then the Military took over the government, claiming irregularities at the polls. At the moment things are not looking bad at all. Indications are that the Army is honest about planning a clean election and getting out.

In Canada in the area in Montreal where my family have their home, it is reported that a Cuban-trained terrorist is responsible for the bombing of post-boxes and military buildings, resulting in the death of an innocent old man and the maiming of an army sergeant. It seems incredible that such things should happen in a place so far removed from the sort of misery that is breeding Communism in so many of the countries in this part of the world. Here in Peru university students trained in Cuba have been involved in some skirmishing in isolated mountain areas, but we are told

106

that terrorist and guerrilla activities have been minimal and, if press reports are to be believed, there is no immediate danger of the spread of such activities.

I have just returned from Trujillo where I have spent three of the most interesting and profitable days of my life. Together with three men chosen from the parish I attended a *'Cursillo de Cristianidad'*. This closed retreat was a unique experience such as comes only once in a lifetime and it seems impossible to find words that can describe it. The silence and penance of the first night change by the morning of the first day into a spirit of common joy that is infectious. Perhaps on another occasion, after I have seen some of the results here in Monsefú, I shall be able to say more. The people who attended came from many different walks of life. We had among us the conductor of the Symphony Orchestra of Trujillo; a pathologist who taught at the University; the president of the university students' organization of Peru who had recently returned from a concentration camp where he had been interned as a supposed Communist; an elderly poet, and many others. The three who came from Monsefú were parents of children in the parish school. One is an Air Force technician, another a farmer and the third a carpenter. At the start very few of these people were more than nominal Catholics, and there were some who were opposed to the Church. The result is known only to God, but it was a wonderful thing to watch. For most of the people there it was the first revelation in their lives of what the Church really means, so that one could perhaps describe them as sleeping Christians. One young student at the close said, "I was only born today!" And he meant it.

MONSEFU, JULY, 1963

The tumult and the shouting are over and Fernando Belaunde Terry is the new president of Peru. We know many fine people who are members of his party and believe his government will be a fair and enlightened one. As for-

107

eigners, of course, and as priests, we have no 'grace of state', as a theologian might put it, to judge what is politically best for Peru. For the country as a whole we hope for a just agrarian reform, technical advice and credit facilities for the small farmer and, in the Civil Service, greater efficiency. For the people of Monsefú we hope first of all the basic services of water and sewerage, the lack of which has cost many lives even since my arrival in the parish.

With satisfaction I must report that I won a little bet on the election, with my confrères. Father Jim and Father John were the losers when the dark horse I had backed won. Father John's well-known shrewd sense of political realities suffered a set-back proportioned only to the satisfaction we all felt in the outcome.

We made no bets about the election of the Holy Father because it was too sacred a subject and we shared the world's sorrow on the death of Pope John XXIII. The military transition government of Peru declared a day of mourning and, in homage to the dead Pontiff, all political parties abruptly ended their last-minute appeals to the electorate. Nothing in this country has ever given more hope for the revival of the prestige of the Church — which has suffered greatly over the last century — than the fatherly figure of Pope John. Now we are awaiting the direction of Pope Paul VI whom God has given us in these troubled times.

The election in Monsefú was very orderly. A few days after it was all over one of the elected deputies came to see us to tell us how impressed he had been by the atmosphere of calm in Monsefú on Election Day. It is the custom in this country for the voting to take place on Sunday, and all other gatherings are forbidden on that day. The Hierarchy of Peru had issued the usual directive, stating that Sunday Masses must be celebrated before 8 a.m. or after 6 p.m. So, when Deputy Andres Ezcurra Townsend arrived in town and got the impression that we were chanting the Divine Office in the parish church in large numbers and with great fervour, the truth of the matter was that we were in the hills on a picnic. What he actually heard were the lovely

Upper: Fr. Conroy newly elected mayor of Monsefú. Lower: Fr. Conroy (in white soutane) attending a meeting of school council.

Left: Fr. Conroy on returning from mountain villages a few days before the fatal accident (see p. 187). Right: A *minga* of street repairs Fr. Conroy organized.

Left: Typical transportation with water for sale. Right: Newly dug trenches through town to hold waterpipes Fr. Conroy planned when mayor.

voices of the monks of Solesmes Abbey in France on long-playing records which we had left to be boomed out over the church loud-speaker. Since we didn't have suffrage to vote or sufferance to celebrate Mass we decided we might as well drive the Sisters inland far enough to get a good glimpse of the real mounains. The Sisters of St. Joseph and the Ursulines were joined on the outing by our own Sisters of Mercy, and not a word of politics came up all day. We had left Father Maddigan to man the quiet fort at home and he reported that he had enjoyed our absence very much.

A few days ago Father John returned from Callanca where he had celebrated Mass, bringing with him a young ram which had been given him as *primicias* or first-fruits. This biblical custom is now almost extinct, but it is still practised by one old man up in that part of the parish. Since Father Maddigan is a town product and lived most of his life in a part of St. John's in Newfoundland where no sheep have grazed these hundred years, he thought it was a goat. He brought it home in style in the back seat of the little car and let it loose in the alley-way between church and house. He bought some alfalfa for it and set out drinking water and, since I am off on holiday myself at the time of writing, that's all I know about the ram, except that it doesn't know what to make of us and will probably be short-lived. That same day one parishioner had given us a chicken which wandered into the dining-room from the kitchen and flew into Father John's lap while he was eating. To borrow the language of a character of my acquaintance in a Newfoundland outport, he gave 'a lep like an archangel' and spilled things all over the table. Since we are continually dealing with winged life, both large and small, he should not have been alarmed so easily.

Father John is treasurer of our household and of all our affairs, including the credit union which we have recently got going. There are many credit unions in Peru and a good number in the Chiclayo area. Ours, we hope, will ride in on the coat-tails of the earlier ones. Unfortunately, one important factor for ultimate success is at the present time lacking — an awareness on the part of the members of the full implications of co-operation. Education of the members is of prime importance so as to make them realise that this is their crusade, not ours.

Our ultimate hope here in Latin America is to reach a stage where we ourselves are no longer necessary. This is especially relevant to the co-operative movement which we feel strongly should be in the sphere of the laity.

MONTREAL, CANADA, JULY, 1963.

Just before I left Monsefú for a Canadian holiday Father Jim Doody spent a week visiting some backward coastal parishes in preparation for a pastoral visit of the auxiliary bishop. It involved immense effort and much hard work in giving short courses to innumerable children to prepare them for First Holy Communion and for Confirmation, hearing the confessions of the confirmandi and others and visiting people who seldom see a priest. He fared well on the local food in spite of unhappy forebodings and came home with a fund of information and experience which I hope he will share with me when I get back. I learn from a letter from him that Sister Ana Maria, through patient obedience to doctor's orders, is gaining strength. Her Silver Jubilee as a Sister was celebrated with all the solemnity that Monsefú enjoys giving to such an occasion. In spite of what she would say of herself, she has long been known as the heart of the Community, the most hilarious wit, the best example of obedience to the Rule, the kindest and the most subject to teasing.

I spent an evening with Gerald Clark a couple of days ago. He is an associate editor of the Montreal Star and a fine writer. His most recent book, 'The Coming Explosion in Latin America' is based on personal observation of political and social situations during prolonged visits to a number of the countries that make up Latin America. It is a disturbing book in its analysis of the forces that are building up, inexorably, he feels, to a violent social upheaval which will not be bloodless. It is honest, well-documented and full

110

of interest. I was consoled to learn that what depressed him most, next to the north-east of Brazil where he saw spindly-legged children, marked by malnutrition, working in the fields as cane-cutters at six cents a day, was our own Peru. I would hate to think that there are many countries in the world where slighted human dignity exists to the degree found in the vast Indian population of Peru. During our conversation he told me that he had been offered a second trip to Peru with all expenses paid because, it was indicated, he had not met the right people the first time. Nevertheless, he seems to have done very well in rounding up facts and collecting opinions that would never have been available to him if he had allowed himself to be treated as a V.I.P., or if he had moved solely within the charmed circle of the wealthy, cultured, land-owning families.

MONSEFU, AUGUST 12TH, 1963

Since my return to Peru last month the days have been eventful. The biggest noise around here now am I. This is the way it happened:

President Belaunde's electoral promises included a firm undertaking to restore democracy to the country on all levels of government and to decentralize the tax system. The existing system vested all power in the central government in Lima, so that even the mayors of the lesser municipalities in the country held office by appointment and by government favour.

The very day he took office President Belaunde called for municipal elections by acclamation for a term that would only last for six months — until the machinery for voting by ballot could be set up. A committee of citizens came to me to ask if I would let myself be nominated. It was a startling and novel idea as I had never before heard of a priest-mayor, but the chance of getting something done in our town tempted me. I thought about the water tower, so badly needed and so long talked about, and it occurred to me that in six months I could learn much about the workings of the Council — and perhaps in the process the members of the Council would learn something too if I pushed for action.

I went to Chiclayo to see Bishop Figueroa and found him enthusiastic. He felt it would make good propaganda to have one of his gringo priests as mayor of a town that had formerly been known throughout the country as bitterly anti-clerical, and we both agreed that the six months' term of office would not be long enough to be too heavy a burden on me or on the other priests who would have to take over some of my routine duties during the period. And so, at a town meeting held on August 4th, I was acclaimed mayor of Monsefú.

MONSEFU, AUGUST 25TH, 1963

Once the swearing in ceremony was over I felt that swift action might well result in a momentum that would carry us far, so on the following Sunday I called a public meeting after Mass to ask for a pledge of support from the people for a sewage project for the town. Our friend, Dr. Ricardo Ramirez-Gaston, had got in touch with his brother-in-law who is head of The Plan of Government, and had extracted a promise from him that materials for the project would be sent immediately if we could get free labour to lighten the cost for the federal authorities. The response was impressive and so I wrote the President.

Since last writing we have had five plenary sittings of the Council, three in one day, first for the swearing-in, then for the replacement of a member who had resigned because he had not been made Deputy Mayor and one at night to review the duties of each one of the councillors. Later there were meetings to make up commissions to attend to routine business; but all the while we were dealing with matters presented to us for consideration by people within and without the Council. Procedure on these occasions is too complicated to describe here, but I came to the conclusion

112

that it is largely the reason why nothing of note has ever been done by municipalities.

Cardinal Landazari has written Bishop Figueroa saying he doesn't like this idea of a priest-mayor. The bishop has written back saying that Monsefú is unique, that there is no cause for alarm, and assuring him that when the six months' term is up I have no intention of running for office again.

I am to be in Lima on September 10th, the day set for representatives from the Department of Lambayeque, which includes our area, to present their briefs to the President and to ask for discussions of their problems. Meanwhile I have been doing a little research on the cost of the water and sewer project and find that, though it is too costly to be within the scope of present government planning of public works, we have strong support among some influential members of the government for making it a pilot project.

We have Father Bill Cooney with us again, but this time for medical treatment of a gland infection. He has been sent to bed for two weeks and has to be given two needles a day, with Father Jim and myself acting in the rôle of doctors. He never complains but he has confided to Father John that he hopes some day he will be able to return the favour in kind. Last evening we sat at his bedside and, while quaffing from the flowing bowl, cheered him by playing a tape-recording of Newfoundland folk songs which has recently come to us.

The big, September feast of the Captive Lord is coming up and we hope that the work being done on the interior of the church will be completed in time. We are scaling the old plaster off the columns in the church, including much of the mortar between the bricks and are replacing it with a cement sheathing which will better resist the damp and the saltpetre of the bricks. A *baldaquino* will be made for the main altar; the ceiling will be cleaned; weak plaster above the dampness level will be replaced; the whole will be repainted and there will be a complete electrical re-wiring. The cost of these repairs will be met from various sources — the savings of the church societies, funds coming from the Sep-

113

tember feast of the Captive Lord and the generous gift of $1,000 from Bishop Curtis of Bridgeport whose appreciation of our concern for the three priests of his diocese who are now in language school but who will shortly take over the difficult parish of Santa Cruz, left us breathless. It was only natural that we should do what we could for them and him in the way of sharing our experience. In arranging for the installation of a water system that would be a safeguard to health in the house we had rented for them in the mountains, we were only passing on the kindness we had received ourselves, particularly in the first, difficult year of our mission.

MONSEFU, SEPT. 30, 1963

The most important feast of the year in this area is over at last — that of *El Senor Cautivo*, the Captive Lord, and we are all feeling as if our legs were weighted with lead. I got away from it all during the earlier days of the celebrations as I had to be in Lima on Lambayeque Day, September 10th, to attend the conference held by President Belaunde when the needs and problems of this whole northern area were to be discussed. Two hours had been allotted for the conference, but the problems of our district were not admitted for discussion until near the end of that time, and then there was a near-riot for the right to speak. I decided there and then not to force the issue in what would have been a distracted, if not hostile, climate. Our memorandum had gone in through formal channels, and I had been in contact with most of the people who would be involved in our project of providing our town with water and sewerage which is our immediate objective. I also had the support of the Vice-President of the Republic, Edgardo Seone, who had been our guest in Monsefú during Archbishop Skinner's visit. He had intended to introduce me to the Minister of Finance with the idea of discussing the availability of funds for our project as an immediate undertaking. However, when the President came to the conference room it was to announce that Manuel Seone, Edgardo's brother, who had been in

114

Washington as a representative of the Alliance for Progress in the Organization of American States, had died of a heart attack that afternoon in Georgetown Hospital. So Edgardo went to Washington.

Yesterday the President came to Chiclayo with some of his cabinet ministers to inspect a reservoir which is in course of construction and which, when finished, will regulate the irrigation system of this whole area. While he was there I sent him, through my friend, Fernando Seminario, who was called into conference with him, a photograph of the meeting held in Monsefú a few days after the election, showing at least five hundred hands raised in promise to do the digging for the water and sewer project. It had been my hope to get the President to come to Monsefú that day because he is very interested in reviving old community customs of the Indian culture, and this offer of work by the people is in the ancient *Minga* tradition, now dying out. A secondary consideration was that he would never see more dirt anywhere than he would in this town in fiesta time when many hundreds of people come from outlying places and camp in the streets for the duration of the festivities. It is at such a time that the need for basic facilities is most evident. It was a disappointment when the President's many protectors advised against the visit.

Abbé Pierre, whose fame is widespread, came on a visit and spent a night with us during the fiesta time. He was obviously very tired and I was glad he didn't have enough energy to look out his bedroom window at the people sleeping on the concrete of the alley behind the presbytery. He would certainly have been out among them. As it was, his Swedish interpreter hesitated to let him stay with us, fearing his much-needed rest would be shattered by the roar of early morning rockets. I went out into the streets myself at dawn to keep the brass band from coming near our house until the sun was well up and to hold off the super-rockets as long as possible. But at 8.45 the town reverberated as they were touched off. Father Tex Mitchell, who had made an overnight stay with us on his way north, popped out of his room as if he were on the end of one of the rockets, but there was no stir from Abbé Pierre. I looked in on him at ten o'clock and he seemed to be asleep. By this time I was worried. It didn't seem possible that anyone could sleep through the blare of the brass band, punctuated by the thunder of the rockets, and I couldn't help wondering if he had died in his sleep. Along with my concern another thought slid into my mind that was not altogether sad. If such a thing had happened maybe it was a good thing that it had happened to us. We'd surely go down in the books when they canonized him.

At 10.30 he came to and explained that he had lost hearing in one ear during the war and always slept on the other.

MONSEFU, OCTOBER 28TH, 1963

Tomas Tullume, Monsefú's most noted *brujo,* was Public Enemy Number One in my book, and no one knew it better than he. I had refused to let him be god-father to a child or best man at a wedding unless he would first publish in our local paper a renunciation of witch-craft, his main source of income. His legitimate wife would be the easiest of several to leave, so there was little chance that his family life could be improved. When I refused to celebrate Mass for a fiesta of which he was the chief organizer it was an almost mortal blow to his self-esteem, for capital punishment would seem more sweet than that all religious significance should be removed from a feast celebration. After that, every time I saw his baby face under the broad straw hat it was turned carefully away from me.

Two weeks ago the situation changed. That was on a fiesta occasion when we called up the first of our work parties, with the two-fold purpose of fixing up the streets for the celebration of Monsefú's diamond jubilee as a town and of trying out the people who had promised to get out and dig for our hoped-for water and sewer project. Tomas was quick to see an opportunity and to seize it. Of the hundred and twenty men who turned up for the *minga,* Tomas supplied thirty — and a pair of oxen dragging a steel plough

116

to boot. As a priest, I had no hesitation in refusing his participation in things religious, but as mayor, I felt I had no right to refuse his contribution to our civic works program, so Tomas joined forces with us. The following week he repeated the performance, drawing attention to his work contribution by challenging other fiesta organizers to put up a similar squad.

The two days' work done by a hundred and twenty men did not go beyond taking up the flagstones of the sidewalks and the cobblestones of one street block and relaying them after levelling, but it proved what I had known inwardly — that there is still strength in the old customs. In earlier times men would gather in groups to work for a day on some project directed towards a fiesta occasion which might still be many months away. The day selected would usually be Monday, or 'little Sunday' which is regarded as a holiday. The wives would prepare food and send abundant amounts of chicha. The work would go happily to the rhythm of a little flute and drum, played at the same time by the same person. At the close of the day a mayordomo would inquire if they wanted pay for their work. Some would ask for half the day's earnings and others would say "It goes from the heart." The pay not received from the employer would go to them as a group, perhaps ten months later, to help with the cost of the fiesta celebration. In the meantime the employer would have time to reap the reward of the *minga* and would be able to pay up at fiesta time. The custom hasn't quite died and I think we may be able to revive it in an adapted form for the good of this town.

MONSEFU, NOVEMBER, 1963

Last week, on impulse, I sent a telegram to the manager of the International Petroleum Company in Talara, two hundred miles to the north of us, telling him we were living on five centuries of garbage for want of one of their dump trucks, and could they part with one at a cost that we

117

could meet. He replied that he would be glad to sell us a vehicle. So today I went to Talara to represent our Town Council in the purchase of a second-hand dump truck.

Shortly after we came to Monsefú that company had given us a quantity of used furniture which was a tremendous help to us. They are in difficulties now with the government over an old legal dispute, inherited and not of their making, and are in fear of being nationalized. But today I asked no questions, not wanting to get into a hot political controversy but only into a little old dump truck.

The oil town of Talara, under that company's control, is a model of its kind, with good housing, good living conditions and an excellent relationship between management and employees. The staff numbers about two hundred and fifty Peruvian technicians and seventy North Americans. Most of the latter are Canadians from Alberta. The staff dread the prospect of the company's becoming a government operation.

It was to Talara that Father Tom Reilly went after helping us out here in the early days. His first undertaking there was to build a small temporary church, then a school and, latterly, a huge parish hall. And now he has been moved to another parish. He is in Lima at the present time but we are hoping to see him in a few days, as he may come north with the Sisters of Charity who have just arrived and who are to take over the parish school in Talara. The Ursulines in Chiclayo and our own Sisters of Mercy will be the nearest English-speaking communities to them, but within a year I am willing to bet that Sisters from the diocese of Bridgeport, Connecticut, will be working in the mountain parish of Santa Cruz with the priests from that diocese.

The big news today is that it rained last night. The streets were wet this morning and for the whole day there was no dust. The last recorded heavy rain was in 1926, but I recall at least one occasion since I have been on this desert coast when it rained gently, if briefly. Last night the procession of the Lord of the Miracles took place. The rain may have somewhat dampened the enthusiasm of the 'purple people' as they call the men got up in purple gowns to signify their devotion to this Lima picture, but they were still in the streets with massed bands blaring at midnight. It is a matter of wonder to me sometimes that private devotions can make such a mockery of the liturgy.

MONSEFU, NOVEMBER 13TH, 1963

The Monday work-parties are continuing well, and there is a lot of enthusiasm among the people. The favourable publicity the *mingas* brought us resulted in our getting six wheelbarrows, eighteen shovels and sixty pick-axes from the government on indefinite loan. With these tools we'll be able to warm up for the big dig for the sewer project for which as yet there is no money available.

Father Jim and Father John have been without much help from me latterly in parish visiting, since I have been too embroiled in civic affairs to share in this work. The new school, too, which got off to a slow start because of delays in getting specifications, has taken much of my attention, and also the work being done on the interior of the church. No one seems to mind that we ripped out eleven side-altars and transformed the whole interior. They all want to be modern, but every move on our part must be made with caution to avoid giving any unnecessary offence. The church itself is a fine structure with walls five feet thick of mud brick and fired brick. It has a light cane roof sealed with dried mud and covered with a wooden ceiling in sections on which are depicted, between the arches, scenes representing the sacraments. This is all we have left untouched.

All the wooden altar-pieces have been taken out and their bases of stone and brick have been removed, together with the wooden or iron railings which enclosed them. There is much more room in the church now, with nothing to jar the eye or interfere with movement. The sacristy is crowded with statues, most of which will be put back later in niches now being carved in the deep walls. "Enough for a good game of football," was the irreverent comment of a visiting colleague as he looked over the collection of statues.

119

I am on my way to Talara to bring home the dump truck purchased from the International Petroleum Company, which was to be checked and overhauled before delivery. At the same time I am planning to have a day of recollection in Mike Crowley's parish of Nuevo Pueblo, near Piura. It may turn out to be a half-day of recollection, with the other half riot, as the two Irishmen who are giving me a lift will share the visit to Mike. They are Father John Murphy and Father Tim O'Sullivan, both St. James Society men working in Chimbote, a mushrooming town half-way between Chiclayo and Lima, which is growing prosperous on fish-meal products. One of my companions is from Cork, the other from Cloyne and, to the shame of my own Irish heritage, I find I cannot easily understand their soft-spoken conversation.

The past few days have been more than usually hectic with parish affairs and outside commitments. In addition, our presbytery has been a gathering place for many of our friends who know that the latch-string is always out.

Late last month I was away from the parish, high up in the mountains in Santa Cruz, confirming the arrangements about the house the Bridgeport priests were to occupy, and seeing to it that the place would be fit to live in. As I crossed the main square of the town I heard some high-school youngsters say, "Pobre Kennedy! Pobre Kennedy!" At first I thought they were saying, "Pobre Canada!" trying to rile me, associating me with the American priests. Anti-U.S. sentiments are not usual in our own area, but we run into them from time to time. When I heard more and the news sank in that I was hearing of the assassination of President Kennedy, I was more shaken than I could have believed possible. Later, I tried to think about it with the mind and not with the heart, weighing the pros and cons of his personality and his career. Father John Horgan who had been critical of him since the coup against the Nhu family in Indochina, was so shocked that he could think of nothing else for days. The priests offered Mass for him. The people had an awareness that his death was momentous and talked of nothing else. I found myself surprised at how deeply I was affected personally by his death.

We had the bishop out last Saturday for five hundred confirmations and, in the same week, we had nearly as many first communions. We also had a talk given to the assembled clergy on pastoral and social conditions in Monsefú. It led to discussion afterwards in which argument waxed hot. I stepped aside and let the others fight it out about the cult of statues and the pros and cons of extra services for the dead. The bishop ended the argument by upholding my opinion — which made me respect him ever so much more, of course.

Last Sunday I gave the sermon at the biggest annual feast in the parish of Mochumi. It was an honour to be asked on such an occasion by one of the local native secular priests. So I'm riding on the pig's back these days and can do no wrong.

DAYS LATER.

I am back in Monsefú again, without having mailed my letter. Somewhere along the way I lost the envelope and stamps I was carrying. When I got to Talara the dump truck was not ready but at least they are fixing it up. Next Monday Father Dave Beckerer (successor to Father Tom Reilly as pastor) will drive it down to us. I came back with the priests from Cork and Cloyne, letting them monopolise the conversation so that I would have a better chance of understanding what they were saying. John Murphy was born the day the Black-and-Tans burned Cork. The celebration got out of hand, he says. He is forty-three and Father Sullivan a bit younger. The Irish brigade of the St. James Society is growing quite large. Mike told me that at his suggestion Bishop Lucey of Cork had asked Cardinal Cushing to let the men from Cork organize along the lines of our set-up in Monsefú, but the Cardinal wants to bear the whole financial burden of the St. James Society and have the control of it. That dispensation can only be temporary because not even Cardinal Cushing and Boston can support such a rapidly growing organization. It is already obvious in the economic strain they are all feeling.

We had a happy visit in Mike's parish. The morning was spent before the Blessed Sacrament exposed. Then, at lunchtime, Father Dick Walsh made Manhattans, Fathers Crowley and Lohan cooked steaks and poured Chilean wine — and the desert bloomed. The rapid-fire conversation over Society policy among the eight priests present was very interesting. Later in the afternoon we went down to the beach in the resort of Colan where, at this hottest time of year, there are as many as twenty private planes and a string of summer cabins owned by wealthy families. Last summer I wouldn't know what sting the families feared most — the sting-rays that are plentiful in the salt water or the sermons on social encyclicals they got when they went, devout, to Mass.

The three priests from the Bridgeport diocese are finally established in Santa Cruz. They spent a week with us before they set out.

The day after tomorrow a new mayor will be elected. Three candidates are running, but this time as a priest I am automatically excluded by a law recently passed which excludes also military men and civil servants. The past six months have been frustrating, but I suppose it was all worthwhile. Our struggle to get public services in the town is continuing, but without commitment yet on the part of the government. I can still engage in that battle through the Monsefú Development Junta which is officially recognized and of which I am president.

The Monday *mingas* must continue or else the town will go back to its eternal sleep. The government is willing to pay for a water tower this year, but we want much more than that. We may be able to get them to supply the materials needed for a sewage system, but even so, that would mean that our people would have to supply the labour (or the money) required for the trenches that would carry the pipes through the town and perhaps all the way to the sea and for making the concrete pipes with material supplied. It will require patient education of the people, but it will be worth it if the government does its part. I am sure that if nothing is done this year, the opportunity will be lost and it will be ten years or forever before Monsefú will get essential basic services.

On the way north to Talara last week with my two Irish friends we had lunch with Edgardo Seone and his family at their farm near Chiclayo. I was interested to find that he had just returned from a visit to Spain, Italy, Israel, Brazil and Mexico, in all of which countries he had seen the results of various efforts at redistribution of farmland. As Vice-President of Peru he had talked with Pope Paul for half an hour and was impressed by the Pontiff's clear understanding and great goodness. They talked mostly about social conditions in Peru and the problem of land reform. Seone had been delegate to the first World Congress of the Lay Apostolate about ten years ago, but he had never known Pope Paul.

I told him I was on my way to Talara, the oil city, to pick up a dump truck which the Municipal Council in Monsefú had bought from the International Petroleum Company for four hundred dollars. "Will they get it?" he grinned. I asked him then how things were going in the dispute between the Company and the Government. He said that if the American Government was withholding Alliance for Progress funds from Peru for the purpose of forcing a settlement with the International Petroleum Company, it would be a sad example of reversion to old-style imperialist diplomacy. In such case, he said, Peru would have to manage on its own.

I had no expectation of hearing the arguments on the other side of this controversy but thirty-six hours later I came in from Mass in the parish of Talara to find that the manager of the International Petroleum Company, William Nugent, and other top company officials had just called on the pastor, Father Dave Beckerer, bringing a four thousand dollar contribution towards the parish building program. They stayed for a cup of coffee and I talked to Nugent

123

about the dump truck which will soon be ready to roll. I also spoke about my conversation with Edgardo Seone. He said the situation looks grim for the company. They would like to make a settlement with the government over a long-existing tax deal which greatly favours the company but which was made in times of disorganized rule in the country, but they cannot see themselves paying the astronomical amount the present government asks. I feel that since good people are involved on both sides, a just solution will eventually be reached.

How did I get into politics again, when I am just getting out of them on the municipal level? Excuse me.

MONSEFU, JANUARY, 1964.

Father Hector Effio, a newly-ordained Dominican priest, came home recently to Santa Rosa to see his parents and to offer his First Solemn Mass. This is a harvest out of season, coming well before its time, and not one that was sown by us. There never was a happier day for us in Santa Rosa than the day of his First Mass, and it was a joy for himself as well to give Holy Communion to his own parents. From them he had received many natural virtues, although his vocation to the priesthood did not stem from home or family surroundings. He had left home at the age of fourteen and had somehow managed to get an education on his own. He had held many different jobs and had served for a time in the armed forces. While working as a hospital attendant he came in contact with the Dominican Order in Lima — the same Order that claims as a member of nearly four hundred years ago another Peruvian, St. Martin de Porres. He was the only one to persevere of eleven Peruvians sent to the Dominican Scholasticate in Colombia and, on his ordination, was given permission by the General of the Order to come home for a visit. Such permission is significant because the Peruvian Province of the Order is going through troubled times because of friction between native and foreign mentalities.

Father Hector talked to his own people as a group and individually. He said the very things we have been trying to get across to them for years, but in a way which reached them. His presence, quite as much as his efforts, resulted in the fixing up of a number of marriages that were irregular, although in the matter of the Sunday obligation to attend Mass he was no more successful than we were ourselves. Even his own parents were absent from the second mass he celebrated which was on the Sunday before Christmas. It is an obligation that we have never been able to get the older people to accept. However, a great many young people came to the sacraments during the first days of Father Hector's visit and the dictum that a prophet is not without honour, save in his own country, proved to be true only in its application to Sunday Mass.

One day during Father Hector's stay I went with him to the First Annual Meeting of the Maritime Society of Fishermen where he spoke for nearly two hours. The morning session ended at three in the afternoon, without even half the business on the agenda having been dealt with. As he talked on and on, I began to wonder if the members would take him bodily and drop him outside somewhere so that they could get on with the business in hand. In spite of all, however, they agreed to go fishing for the church en masse — something that had never happened before in Santa Rosa's history. It was decided that fourteen boats, each with a crew of eight, would go out after *bonito* on January 7th. I have not yet heard how they made out because I only got back from a fishing expedition myself on the morning of that day and left almost immediately for Lima.

At this time of year the fishermen of Santa Rosa undertake three types of fishing expeditions: (a) To the Islands, a two-day trip; (b) To 'the big nets', an overnight voyage; (c) To the 'mono', an all-day undertaking from six in the morning until late afternoon.

On the Feast of the Epiphany, at 4 o'clock in the afternoon, Father Hector, Father Jim Doody and I joined the crew of a fishing boat for a trip to the big nets. I took the movie camera which Monsignor Summers had left with us, to record the scene. The incongruity of this did not prevent thoughts of the Sea of Galilee from coming to mind.

It took us more than half an hour to push the boat down the sand and into the breakers with logs for rollers and ten men helping. Once out in the water, beyond the surf, there was nothing further we could do to help. The boat was named 'Freedom of Peru', one of the few which do not have religious names. I had been told that it was named 'Girl in every Port' and had wondered how that would look in our pictures.

The net was of nylon, about forty feet wide and half a mile long. One edge was weighted with lead sinkers, while circles of cork were strung along the other, thus making it possible for it to stand upright in the water. When soundings through the oar (a primitive but effective way of locating the presence of a school of fish) indicated that we were in a good spot, the net was uncoiled and let down twenty fathoms until it rested on the ocean floor. Our station for the night was determined by the first buoy and anchor marking the position of the net. We came back to it after setting the net and took up the buoy.

At twilight a school of porpoises came frolicking by on some happy mission of their own. They had no fear of us nor, for that matter, were they even interested in us, but rushed on hell-for-leather, concerned only with some porpoise purpose of their own. There were pelicans and gulls too, and a little bird that hovered only long enough to sip at a bubble of oil on the water. Just before the brief twilight turned suddenly to night, we had a 'mug-up'. Father Jim began to calculate, as he so often does at odd moments, just where his friend, Father Denis Walsh, back in Newfoundland, would be at this time. We ourselves were feeling most appreciative of the kindness of the Peruvian climate as we recalled what it would be like to be anchored in a fishing boat off the coast of Newfoundland on a January night. Having decided that this was not Father Walsh's present fate, we turned in and went to sleep under the stars on a carpet of rushes.

At 1 a.m. the skipper of our craft, Moises Santisteban, got us up and began to haul in the net. We had a good catch of *suco,* and *toyo* in abundance. The former is a fine-tasting fish that reveals its presence on the bottom by the noises we had heard through the oar — loud enough at times to keep the fishermen awake. The *toyo* is like the dogfish that Newfoundland fishermen regard with loathing for the damage it does their nets, but this species has no teeth. It also brings a good price and, in spite of its menacing appearance, is regarded as a table delicacy. It is doubtful if the dogfish found on the Atlantic coast will ever be so rated.

By 3 a.m. the net was safely aboard and we set out for home. Between 4 and 6 a.m. we drifted off the Santa Rosa coast while the other fishing boats gathered round. Just before dawn the boats, one after another, went skimming in towards the beach on the crest of a breaker.

Father Maddigan had left the little car on the beach for us, but before we returned to Monsefú we went with Father Hector to choose a site in Santa Rosa which he assured us the local council was willing to give in hope of having a convent and school there some day. Then, damp and fishy, we set out for Monsefú. It had been a most interesting experience and, thanks to Father Hector and our closer contact with the people, perhaps the beginning of better things in Santa Rosa.

LIMA, JANUARY 23RD, 1964.

I am here in Lima, supposedly for a Pastoral Week, following a week's holiday in the mountains, but the conferences are not getting my undivided attention because there are so many things to be done that can only be done here. There are others, too, that cannot be done even here, a discovery that I keep making over and over again the hard way, after much time has been wasted in trying.

Part of my time in Lima has been spent shopping around for new ideas and new ways of getting things done. I have had no luck with AID (Alliance for Progress), the Peace

Corps, or two Peruvian volunteer groups, in getting statistical studies done, or an engineering map, or help in the Monsefú sewage project. Now that I have escaped from the job of being mayor, I have been wondering to what extent I should involve myself in the material side of things. I don't want to drop the *mingas*. There is good physical exercise in that as well as opportunities for friendly contact with the otherwise inaccessible men of the parish. Apart from its good social effect on the community, the practical results justify its continuance.

A few days after my return home from Talara last month our good friends, Father Rudy Masciarelli and Father Dave Beckerer, arrived triumphantly, when least expected, driving the dump truck. It is now in the possession of the Municipal Council, overhauled, painted and in good condition. They saved money on that truck through the generous deal given them by the International Petroleum Company and, as a result, were able to pay off a portion of the debt owed the City of Chiclayo for some years of public lighting.

Unfortunately when I stepped down from the office of mayor, the bigger issues were still untouched. Pressure was brought to bear on the Government to include in the budget for 1964 as much as is feasible for a water and sewer project in Monsefú. The budget, which should have been brought down two months ago, is still being kicked around in Parliament. We'll get a water tank, and maybe some water pipes, but it seems the sewage system will have to wait. If we don't keep shouting it may have to wait for many years.

The new mayor is pledged to carry out the program we started. He depends on my opinion in many things so for the moment I am a Grey Eminence. Our latest project is to detour the big irrigation canal which passes along by the convent and school and the whole southern part of the town. It would be an under-statement to say that it is a hazard to health. I can smell it now, just at the thought of writing about it. Dead animals, human waste, garbage from the homes float in it. Yet the kids swim in it and nearly everyone drinks it.

We received a cheque for five thousand dollars from St. John's a little while ago. This will give us enough to finish the two six-classroom wings of the new school, supplying them with drains, water and electricity. We know this extra amount from the archdiocese, in addition to the sum of fifteen thousand dollars which Archbishop Skinner left with us to get the school building started, was not easy to give, and that wrapped up in a great many of those dollars are the sacrifices of many individuals.

The trip into the mountains was not, perhaps, the holiday I needed most. I was not there long enough to get accustomed to the rarified air and, although it was good to renew old acquaintances, I continued to be light-headed and without appetite or energy even after the faint headache of the first few days wore off. I am a salt-water dog, I am sure. We were at an altitude of about 11,000 feet in Cuzco, Puno and La Paz and I longed for a breath of salt air.

The *Semana Pastoral* is over. I found it interesting, not so much for the discussions, many of which I missed, as for the people who attended. There were a great many new faces and pleasant reunions with friends whose work is established, and from many different countries: Spain, France, Italy, Germany, Belgium, the United States, Canada, Mexico. I had to speak Spanish to most of the Canadians because I have lost my French. The Oblates who are strong in Chile and Bolivia have, up to recently, been weak in Peru. But now they have chosen this country as the one Latin-American mission field for their new English-speaking province. In my list of nations above I forgot to mention Ireland, although there are at least a dozen difficult parishes on the bank of the Rimac in Lima run by Columbans who are for the most part Irish — with a scattering of Australians and a few English-speaking secular priests helping them. And then there is the contingent with the St. James Society. They have three English priests with them also — and one Welshman.

I flashed our simple uniform of a white sports shirt with a Celtic cross stitched in red on the pocket, at the pastoral week conference. It certainly makes for easier communication with people. And in these countries one cannot lessen respect for the cloth by not wearing it, because there isn't any respect to begin with. Not long ago when I gave a few talks in the Chiclayo gaol where I showed film strips with sound recording, I was the more welcome for not looking too clerical. An immediate sign of appreciation came in a gift of some beautifully carved things in bone. Whose bone, I wonder? About a hundred shirts with Celtic crosses in red on the pocket have been turned out in our little Chinese factory for other parishes along the coast.

Tomorrow I expect to drive north to Monsefú in the Sisters' station wagon, bringing eighteen shovels to add to our store, two packages of Legion of Mary handbooks, a new tabernacle with bronze doors back and front, one Irishman and two or three Boston Bolivians.

MONSEFU, FEB. 20TH, 1964.

The clinic we opened in the presbytery is struggling along, but the problem is to get medical supplies. At the end of January we had nothing left but a few aspirins and some ointments. Then when we didn't even have a barrel to scrape the bottom of, we were sent a supply of medicines from Abbé Pierre's Emmaus in Chiclayo. In fourteen months' time we are to be on the list for medical supplies of a Catholic agency in the U. S., and then things will be better. In the meantime we have to scramble for samples from doctors' offices and beg from drug houses. Our greatest need is for antibiotics and some simple, less costly remedies for children's illnesses. Gifts of medical supplies from friends in Canada have been sent, but either have not reached us at all or have been held up for months by Customs complications. With an average of twenty-five patients a day coming to the clinic, the need for supplies is growing desperate.

Every day one of us takes a run into town to bring back an intern from the Chiclayo hospital for our little clinic. Today's man didn't come. Among those waiting was a mother and her baby. I noticed around the infant's neck something that looked as if it might be a fetish, so I asked the mother what it was. She told me it was a skunk's paw — to ward off the evil eye. She added that some people have an evil eye, though they may not be aware of it themselves, that affects only children, making them cry and refuse to eat or sleep. Since it has to be the right forepaw of the animal and skunks are mercifully scarce in these parts, it must be a costly cure. The same little woman got scapulars from me last year to put on her twins, but it seems now she thinks skunks are better.

We had the Mother General and a Mother Provincial of the Nazareth Sisters down here recently to start a foundation in Santa Cruz. They went up into the mountains full of the missionary spirit and came down too frightened to sleep. It was the road that scared them, not the enormity of the undertaking. It had started off as a flat, smooth ribbon of asphalt. Then it became a scenic route with many bumps and twists in it; then it crossed a divide and became a narrow, boulder-strewn, cliff-hugging contortion. In the final lap, beyond the town of Catache, it became a muddy rut, seeded with 'sunkers' and impassable even to trucks. It is a worse road, as I can tell from knowledge of both, than the one by which Gerald Clark made the journey to Vicos which, he said, left him more terrified and shaken than he had been even by wartime shellfire.

Once in Santa Cruz one goes 'pie ajano' (on another's feet) by horse or mule. Some road-building is being attempted between different, isolated towns, so it may happen that different parts of the parish will be joined by routes that can hardly be described as roads, but that will at least make communication possible.

Yesterday morning I went with Father Paul Mooney to Mocupe where he is now pastor. We discussed improvements he is making in his church, then went on to Cayalti to his plane. We flew over Monsefú and its environs and I took about thirty pictures of the area where we hope to re-route the irrigation canal; also of the parish land called 'San Pedro' — two hundred and fifty acres of mostly sand-

dunes which are to be divided up and sold in what we hope
will be a co-operative scheme. He dropped me off in the
desert near the Santa Rosa road and I walked home in about
forty minutes, collecting a good appetite on the way.

MONSEFU, APRIL 1964.

The third anniversary of the coming of the Canadian
priests to Monsefú passed quietly enough. To the people
the date was less a reminder of the beginning of our Mission than of the tragic railway accident that took the lives of
twelve farm workers the day after our arrival. Wrought-
iron crosses are now being erected on the site near the railway tracks where Father Morse and I ministered to the
dying that day. It was our first, sad service to the community.

While the people continue to mourn the twelve who died
violently, they are not greatly stirred at the thought of the
three hundred and more who have died since then from
avoidable causes. I am reminded of St. Augustine's comment
on today's Gospel to the effect that much thought is often
centred on the unusual, but important things can go un-
noticed if they happen often enough to be taken for granted.
Giving that thought a little twist, I feel that it is little short
of miraculous that Monsefú should in recent years have
escaped massive epidemic and plagues. Its history is full of
such cataclysmic occurrences. The figures I have given
above are impressive and sad but are far below plague pro-
portions.

We are now conducting our third annual visit to the
homes of our parishioners. Father Jim came back the other
day with a story of a visit to a home where he found an
eight-months-old baby asleep on a bare earth floor, its little
face covered with flies and fish-bones protruding from its
mouth. Surprisingly, the sturdy little body, where it could
be seen through the dirt, indicated that it was gloriously
healthy. But there are some pitiful little ones, too. We see
many of them when people come in the afternoons to see

the doctor and when dying children are brought to us for baptism. The interns who come from the hospital in Chiclayo to give free services five days a week are better doctors than most of the local practitioners who have given up studying.

Besides the Chiclayo interns and our good friend, Dr. Ricardo Ramirez-Gaston, we are soon to have the help of an orthopaedic specialist, Dr. Humberto Boggiano, who is at present completing his training at the Montreal Children's Hospital in that city. He is planning to return next month to his home town of Chiclayo and has offered already to help us in any way he can. He will be a welcome addition to our team.

The first day of April is school-opening day down here, not a day for practical joking. 'Inocentes', December 28th, is the day for that sort of thing. Many people from Chiclayo are trying to get their children registered in our new school which is at last ready, but this is a time when we have to discriminate against the rich. If we let people in from outside the parish the effect on the Monsefú community will be greatly weakened — and we are hoping for tremendous things. Our Sisters, at the time of writing, are still in Lima taking further language courses, but they should be back very soon.

Our church is beginning to be a place of pilgrimage. It has been repaired and painted within. Niches carved in the thick walls give extra space. Even the confessionals have been set into the walls. The main altar has been moved down closer to the centre of the church — and closer to the people. The 'mensa' or altar table is of Peruvian marble and is supported by columns of stone. The cross over the altar hangs from the ceiling. It was designed and constructed for us in Lima and is extremely beautiful. On one side, set into rough mosaic, are symbols of the Passion — the rooster, sun and moon, flagellum, etc. The 'Corpus' of Our Lord is in wood, carved in low relief. The halo and edges of the cross are finished in gold-leaf. On the other side, facing the shorter end of the church, are symbols of the Resurrection, and here the figure of Christ is shown in majesty. These improvements, made possible partly by contributions in one way or another from the people themselves and partly by gifts from friends for that purpose, might seem at first to be sheer luxury. I feel that they will serve an educational rôle, for no one can fail to see that the altar is the focus of attention and is testimony of the love of Christ for men, the very *raison d'être* of the parish.

We should keep a guest book. Although we are not even shown on some maps, yet visitors find us. The Ursulines in Chiclayo hardly see a day go by without feeding some hungry priest in transit, and we hardly see a night go by without harbouring him. We cannot claim credit for charity in this for, nearly always, it is an English-speaking priest and a friend. Maybe he comes from one of the St. James' parishes, or from Santa Cruz, Mocupe, Cayalti-Zana, or perhaps a Columban or an Oblate from the slums of Lima. Our most recent visitor was Father Tom Curran, C.S.C. from the Hacienda Cartavio, a huge commercial farm three hours' travel south of us. The situation is very often complex on the haciendas which are really little totalitarian states where no one has any land of his own, nor any independence.

With people living on hacienda land in thousands, it is important that priests also should be there to serve them; but they must accept the situation as they find it which, in some cases, means that they minister to parishioners who are no more than serfs in a social environment that is almost medieval. Cartavio is not in this category, however. It is owned by the Grace Company and it was Peter Grace who persuaded the Holy Cross Fathers to come there; so they get every co-operation from the management in caring for the twenty thousand people who live and work there.

MONSEFU, APRIL 1964.

Small victories made for a more peaceful and recollected Holy Week than Monsefú has known for years. Two dances were called off, one on Palm Sunday that had been planned by the Municipal Council and one on the night of Holy

Saturday which had been organized by a football team known as 'The Apostles'. Monday's Holy Week procession was cancelled also. On Wednesday night the statue of the Lord of the Seven Falls was carried around the park in front of the church instead of getting lost in the narrow and buckety streets. That was achieved, not without a struggle and a dragging out of the time from four hours to five. The music of the band has an absolutely hypnotic effect at these times. The men who carry the *anda* or platform on which the statue is placed, by means of poles resting on their shoulders, sway back and forth to the sad beat for many long minutes between one step and the next.

Holy Thursday was a day of many consoling confessions and a better turnout than we had ever seen before. In the morning two of us represented the parish at the Mass of the Oils in the Cathedral in Chiclayo, while two Vincentian priests came out to help with confessions here. Before the evening Mass I gave a hand in our neighbouring parish of Eten and was impressed by the good confessions. Just the same, I was glad of the changes we had made in Monsefú when I saw how things were in Eten. A procession of Our Lady of Sorrows came into the church and marched down the aisle with the band playing at full blast. The Altar of Repose was being prepared in the sanctuary while a canvas screen which was not quite long enough cut off the view of the sanctuary from the main part of the church. The result was that the floor was carpeted with several dozen children, lying on their stomachs and kicking up their heels while they watched in fascination the preparations from under the canvas. In all this chaos there is something endearing. At the entrance to the church, for instance, a banquet was arranged to represent the Last Supper. Fruit and real food were on the table around which were placed thirteen statues holding partly peeled bananas in their hands. For the most part they were ones taken out of storage, of now-forgotten saints, and most of them were tonsured Franciscans. One of the loaves on the table was in the shape of the Paschal Lamb. The custom is quaint, but I am sure that its meaning is long forgotten here.

135

Our Good Friday procession went well, although it took just as long to go around the square as in an earlier year it had taken to go around the town, even with carefully chosen *cargadores*, each of whom wore a white ribbon over his dark suit. By means of a portable loud-speaker we could make ourselves heard through the music and could lead prayers that gave some meaning to the procession and made the music less hypnotic. So, news of the Resurrection is filtering through.

MONSEFU, APRIL 5TH, 1964

The news got around that I was having a birthday and I wasn't allowed to forget it. Several times a day the radio could be heard blasting 'Happy Birthday to You' in unctuous tones in English — as is done for any who are celebrating their 'onomastic date'. Birthdays are big events down here. They are usually referred to as 'The Day of your Saint' because of the custom of giving children names according to the feast day of their birth. If the liturgy, in its temporal cycle, overpowers the saints, the child may be called Ramos, Cruz, Ascencion or Manuel — in reference to Palm Sunday; a feast of the Cross; the Ascension; or Christmas. One little fellow, between six and seven years of age, gave me the customary pat on the back — as high as he could reach — and recited me a speech his parents had taught him. A parishioner who is our prize neurotic sent over a chicken. It had no feathers from the wings up and I thought she had in kindness done half the plucking for us with the creature still alive; but others assured me that this is its nature. It was considerate of her, too, to send it in a plastic bag which leaked nothing but the warmth of the bird. It is perched, quietly pensive, outside my window as I write.

The Alaskan earthquakes were felt down here in high tidal waves. We were on the beach a few days ago near our favourite wreck, the 'Santa Fe', when a great wave came slopping along casually, sideways, and made us jump for higher ground. Watch, breviary, camera, were all saved,

136

and only a magazine lost. On the way home afterwards we met convoys of trucks coming from Monsefú. Word of a tidal wave brought all the people out in the streets. We had about ten kids hanging on to our car, waving at the crowds and shouting, "It's nothing — nothing at all!" Behind us in another car was the *brujo*, Tomas Tullume. We still don't know which of us was given the credit for turning back the sea.

MONSEFU, APRIL 24TH, 1964.

This morning was spent with an engineer from the Irrigation Office in Chiclayo and several others, working out on paper what will be the new course of the irrigation canal. The polluted water of this canal is not only an offence to the sense of smell. It is also a grave menace to the health of the community and, specifically, is the cause of much illness and many deaths. It brings not only industrial waste and town sewage periodically from the Hacienda Pomalca, but also takes the waste from the hundred or more homes built along its borders. My function in this matter is to get a united front of those who are aware of the danger and want to do something about it against others with authoritative opinions who have no interest in the common good. It will be a struggle, but with persistence and a little luck I think the project will be realised.

Yesterday was a memorable day in the life of Father Jim Doody when he saved a drowning man's life and nearly lost his own in the doing of it. He had been sitting quietly on the beach reading his breviary, but decided to go in for a swim. Just as he got through the surf he saw a man struggling in panic in the water. He reached him in seconds, but before he could get his hands on him the man, in his fright, locked his legs around Jim's and grabbed him around the shoulders, pinioning one arm. With only the other arm free to use, he tried to persuade the fellow to slacken his grip, but this could only be done between one wave and the next. He doesn't know how he managed it, but at last he reached

137

standing ground and got the victim to shore. Then, for five minutes the two sat on the sand, retching and bringing up salt water. Finally, the man whose life had just been saved got up and limped off, giggling hysterically. Two men detached themselves from a group on the beach and came over to thank Jim. They were from a seminary in Chiclayo operated by the Church of the Nazarene, a Protestant denomination formerly known as the Pentecostal Church of the Nazarene. There were five Americans among them. The rescued man was one of their number. He was from the mountains and, being unused to the sea, had no idea of its force.

I could not help but be glad that it was Father Jim who had been 'called' because, if I had been the one, there would either have been a double drowning or — and this is perhaps more likely — I would have been torn by remorse for the rest of my life for failing to rescue the man. My impulse now is to put up a sign on the beach in English, Quechua and Spanish and perhaps Aymara: "No Life-Saving Allowed!" — a modest proposal that might discourage the foolhardy from endangering their own lives and the lives of others.

MONSEFU, JUNE 6TH, 1964.

Tomorrow morning Project DIG (Diversion of the Irrigation Germ factory — I mean canal) will be undertaken, with Top Brass officiating. The trench is to be over a mile long. It will be ten feet across at the top, with a floor six feet across and a depth of three feet. Tractors will be needed to fill in and level the last part of the course.

A number of important people are in on this project. The Prefect of the Department of Lambayeque, the equivalent of a Lieutenant Governor of a province in Canada, will be here tomorrow to turn the first sod in the digging operation. With him will be the Engineer in charge of Irrigation for all Peru who happens to be in Chiclayo and who has promised a contribution from his office of six to eight hundred dollars towards the bulldozer costs. The little railway that

138

passes through Monsefú on the way to the sea will have to have its line shored up to let the canal pass beneath. The Company concerned will have its representative there to-morrow to take charge of the railway bridge operation. The Planning Junta for the Department of Lambayeque of which our Junta of Local Development is an extension, has made a special visit to Monsefú to study and later to approve the project.

Permission has been granted by most of the owners of the land along the new route, and others have agreed to let water pass through their land to neighbours whose fields are too high for water to reach them by the new, lower route. Local experts, 'practical men', as they are called, will supervise the digging. The engineer from the Office of Irrigation in Chiclayo who made the plan for us will super-vise its execution in his spare time, without charge. All this will be an example of what the government calls *Coopera-cion Popular,* with the people taking initiative or going along with government plans on a fifty-fifty cost basis. In this case we cannot estimate what the cost will be, as any owner of land could demand recompense for allowing the new course of the canal to go through his property. We are hoping enough public spirit will be generated to carry the project through at low cost.

The panic-catastrophe that occurred recently in the foot-ball field in Lima took a frightful toll in lives, as I am sure the press reports have shown. Two boys from Monsefú were among the victims, and there would be few parts of the country that were not represented among the hundreds who died. As with death everywhere in Peru, these deaths were all the sadder for being completely unnecessary. Peruvians are not by any means aggressive, in spite of much provoca-tion at times, but in any nation mob emotion can unleash terrible forces. Added, in the present instance, was the un-forgivable action of the police in firing tear gas into the stands and the underground passages to the exits — and the supreme negligence of having the exits locked!

We are thinking of waging all-out war at the first proved case of rabies; and rabies will come, as it does every month or two to one or another of the nearby pueblos. Dogs here are not pets, except as puppies, and have no other function than to bark. In this town where the houses hug one another at twenty-foot intervals from one front door to the next; where there are no doors inside; where usually as many as fifteen children mill about, the younger ones crawling, eating and sleeping on the earth floor among the chickens and guinea-pigs, I think we are justified in having less compassion for dogs than people.

Reverend Mother Assumpta's recent visit to her Monsefú community brought us all great joy, particularly as she was so very pleased herself with what she found here. It takes someone from outside to see changes that a year has brought that we have hardly noticed ourselves. She was given a wildly enthusiastic reception and at the end of her visit a tremendous send-off.

During Reverend Mother's visit the Sisters were very busy in school, but she found to her delight that the tots could converse with her in English fairly easily and, of course, she herself has picked up enough working Spanish to get along. Her visit was the greatest event of the year for the Sisters and it was crowned by her announcement that they would all be brought home to Newfoundland for Christmas. She feels strongly that these Sisters who were the pioneers in the difficult beginning years of the mission, deserve a real break. The priests are delighted for them also. We have no words that can tell the value of what they have done and are doing to make our own work of permanent value.

The priests also will be in Newfoundland before the end of the year, but not altogether on holiday. We are to return in relays to conduct a campaign for funds in support of the Mission and, in particular, to pay off the second half of the debt His Grace contracted when our presbytery and the school were built. We shall all be back on the job again in Monsefú before the Sisters leave. In the meantime every parish in the archdiocese will be visited by one or another of us and the story of our work will be told. Asking for money will not be an easy task; the only thing that gives it a palatable flavour is that we feel that those who are asked should know something of the life and conditions of the people whose cause we are pleading. Thought of those conditions makes us willing to be beggars.

Father Mike Crowley's three-year term with the St. James Society has ended. He is to return to his home diocese in Ireland this month but we have good reason to think that his bishop may send out a diocesan team of priests, organized along the same lines as our own. If so, Mike will surely head it.

St. Lawrence, Newfoundland, August 17th, 1964

Three years of living along the sandy coastal fringe of Peru which is lapped by the Pacific Ocean had made me almost forget what the sea off the coast of Newfoundland could be like. This visit brings me back to familiar places with a new awareness of life along the shores of home.

Placentia Bay is a place of wild and restless waters. When a boat is not under the *lun* of the land, it heaves with the *scend* from the south-west, though the sky may be holding its breath. Even on such occasional calm days the air is turbulent a league off the land, as if to warn 'No welcome here!' Sunkers and islands are scattered all around the bay and more often than not fog makes navigation difficult. But along the coast there are land-locked coves like Isle Valen — quiet places hidden from the force of the waves. The tidy, oft-painted homes have cosy kitchens where the rage of winter and the whole wide ocean seem of small concern. Even in Little Paradise with its back to a wall of rock and its face to the full force of the sea, homes are warm and snug and bright.

Many of these small and isolated settlements will be abandoned soon for reasons that are good and forceful in a world that is fast changing. It will be hard on the people to go, leaving behind them their homes and fish-stores, wharves and gardens and their familiar fishing grounds that have been won from a rough sea and a rocky land by generations' labour.

141

A quarter of my own being belongs to Placentia Bay and perhaps that is why I could wish some great writer would spend a winter there, living in one of the settlements and carving a story from life out of the rich material to be found there. In a few years' time it will be too late to re-create a life that now seems as old as time but that is already on the way out.

ST. JOHN'S, NEWFOUNDLAND, SEPTEMBER 1964

Father Jim Doody and I have just returned here after a campaign tour of Placentia Bay, St. Mary's Bay and the Southern Shore. We have asked for funds for the Latin-American venture and have found heartening generosity among a people who have themselves in the past known only too well the bitter taste of hard times. For both of us it has been a time of renewal. The welcome we have received and the warmth of the hospitality shown us have given us a lift of heart and spirit. And, believe me, it is not an easy thing to ask for help for people ten thousand miles away whose only claim on Newfoundland is their great need, their common humanity, and the fact that three Newfoundland priests and eight nuns are contributing their help in the effort to repair the wrongs of four centuries of oppression and neglect.

In our campaign for funds for our parish of Monsefú we cannot help noting that those who have given most are those who best remember what poverty is. The whole world knows that the pitiable state of the great majority of people in Latin America is a matter of indifference to the wealthy ruling classes of these countries, and it is easy to condemn the injustice of it all. But there actually does seem to be an alchemy at work, a 'metallizing' influence, a Peruvian would call it, which seems to insulate those who have from those who have not and which makes it hard for those who have possessions and who know so well the pleasures the world has to offer, to have any awareness of the miseries of the under-priviliged, still less to have the urge to alleviate them.

142

Part of the pleasure of our visits to the various settlements has been in noting the changes that have come in the past few years and, in particular, the improvement is basic services — the increased mileage of hard-top road, rural electrification and telephone services, numerous new schools. At the same time, the fragility of the economy of Newfoundland is still evident. We are still too dependent on primary products without guaranteed prices or group security; and there is too much temporary income from ephemeral sources for the future to look as bright as one could wish; and maybe too much money going to Detroit for the lovely cars — the high-cost credit spiderwebs are full of invited guests. But what we find more disturbing than all else is the casual attitude about unemployment insurance and relief — as if the good life should be had for the asking and as a personal, individual right. I would hope that we may never again see the hard old times, but I would pray that we never take abundance for granted.

St John's, October 1964

In a recent issue of Jubilee magazine there is a report from Peru, written by the managing editor, Oona Sullivan. Miss Sullivan writes of 'an astute and knowledgeable Peruvian priest' who is of the opinion that missionaries who come to Peru from North America to stay for two or three years and build churches and set up 'sacramental supermarkets' should stay at home. Her argument is that in most areas of Peru, where local support is negligible, a standard should not be set up that cannot be maintained by the native clergy. This is not a criticism that can be ducked.

Certainly, in our parish of Monsefú, we could not have had the good response that has resulted from our efforts without the strong and constant support of our home archdiocese. How else could we have put up three buildings and maintained a team of three priests and a community of eight nuns? "Let all flowers bloom," said the Chinese poet. It is as certain as it is regrettable that most of what we have accomplished in our parish would be beyond the reach of the Peruvian clergy. Our hope lies in the future. Our aim is to develop a group of young people among whom vocations may be found and who, in any case, should contribute a stimulus of ideas to the rest of the diocese. Other pastoral solutions will be found by other teams of experimenters, be they Belgian, Irish or Peruvian. A revised concept of the missions, a profound reflection on what the Church really is and what it might be, will lead to other experiments. We will stick to what we know we can do well. Our parish school will get a lot of our attention, not because we want to build it in the shape of things at home, but because it is the best answer to the biggest need in our particular situation — the transformation of family life.

ST. JOHN'S, NOVEMBER 1964

The end of September saw Father Jim on his way back to Monsefú and Father John Maddigan on his way to Newfoundland to take his place in campaigning for funds for the Latin-American undertaking. The last days of the campaign were strenuous but gratifying and while we do not yet know the final figures we have every reason to hope that the heaviest portion of the cost of presbytery and school has been realised. Father John and I plan to return together in a few days' time.

Our departure may perhaps remind some people of the story of the outport doctor who returned from a medical convention in St. John's just after a couple of Redemptorist Fathers had left for home on the Mainland, following a Lenten Mission along the coast. The doctor inquired of one of the fishermen if the Mission had gone well. "Begor, Doctor," was the reply, "Be the time them holy men left, there wasn't a mortal sin or a dollar left in the place."

144

This letter is being written in transit to Peru and will be posted from somewhere along the way, probably when the plane touches down at Miami. I am travelling alone as Father John's departure has been delayed for a week or two through an unfortunate mischance. He suffered a second-degree burn on one foot during the celebration of Father Enright's Golden Jubilee, when a trayful of cups of scalding tea cascaded over our missionary. It was a dramatic moment. Those who were present are divided in their reports of Father John's instinctive reaction. Some say he made an utterance that sounded like the beginning of the Act of Contrition, others that it was an unidentifiable yelp of anguish. It is obvious that life can be more dangerous at home than in the mission field. I left him in hospital and went on my way alone.

Archbishop Skinner told me when I saw him shortly before I left St. John's (and just after his return from the Council meetings in Rome) that there had recently been a gathering in Rome of North American bishops who have priests working in Peru, together with Superiors of religious orders who have missionaries there, and with the Peruvian bishops who had come to Rome for the Council meetings. This conference gave expression to the Second Vatican Council's decree concerning the collegiality of bishops — their collective responsibility, in unity with the Pope, for representing the Church's teaching. I was very interested indeed to hear of all this.

On the way through to Montreal for my flight south I saw Bishop Power of Antigonish who has four priests from his diocese working in Central America, with two others in training. They are not working in parishes of their own, but are making an effort to develop local leadership over a broad area. This is the most fundamental work of all because, without local leadership there will be no progress in the economy, no schools, no basis for vocations later. The laity have special competence and 'grace of state' in this field of community development; but when competent laymen are not available, priests must be concerned with it and must devote time to it.

I had the opportunity of speaking on this subject later with Father John McIver of the Scarboro Mission. He is a specialist in community development via co-operatives. He reminded me of Father Jimmie Tompkins' strong conviction that adult education must be given time to 'take root'. He spoke also of his own feeling that the priest should stand back and let the layman 'exercise his own priesthood' by doing what he could to make perfect the world around him. Following these principles, a priest's rôle in community development would normally be the indirect one of fostering lay initiative and leadership. Unless we can do this with the very raw material in Monsefú our work may have no lasting effect, or so it looks to me.

Father Jim who has been holding the fort for us in Monsefú since his return there in September, reports that he has held some *mingas* for road repair recently. Up to the present, with the exception of a small effort by the 'Cesar Vallejo' young people's club, we have not seen the men of our parish turn out completely on their own for any community project. The Local Development Junta of which I am the absent and about-to-retire president, has completed the new irrigation ditch project by reinforcing the walls of the new course and filling in the old. One of the chief figures on this committee, Felipe Reyes, has recently had his four children baptised. This is an early proof of our theory that one thing leads to another and that all things work together for good.

Monsefú has seen the faces of a number of new priest-helpers since the start of our campaign for funds in Newfoundland. During the time that Father Doody was in St. John's and the Placentia Bay area, a Quebec priest of the Fathers of the Blessed Sacrament came to help Father Maddigan. Then came Father Bob Luther and Father George Baldino of the Bridgeport team up in Santa Cruz, taking turns in helping out. Towards the end of our time away from the parish, and until my return, the two new priests of the London diocese have been within range and have made themselves available. They are Fathers Jack Hurley of Sarnia and Vince Gleason from near Chatham, Ontario. They completed their training in mid-November and will be attached to the parishes of Cayalti-Zana and Mocupe in the Chiclayo diocese, together with our former companions, Father Paul Mooney and Father Bill Cooney. To have help when we needed it was most gratifying, but did not come as a surprise. We are all brothers in arms down here.

Our good friend, Dr. Ricardo Ramirez-Gaston, has had much to worry about recently. His small son who attends the Sisters' school, has been very ill with suspected cancer of the bone of one arm. His father wrote me, 'I've had difficult moments with the illness of little Ricardo and I have only got through them with the strength gained in God's Communion which I make each Sunday.' Such a statement would not be out of the ordinary back home but, coming from Peru, it is like the first flower of Spring.

In India, during his visit, Pope Paul appealed to the strong nations to reduce their armaments and divert the resources thus saved to the development of the poor countries of the earth. This proposal gives hope of more competition in the field of foreign aid. And Peru would be one of the first countries to benefit. Already there is a multi-nation effort being made to stamp out world hunger, but it could not be described as a 'race' to accomplish this great good, for there is nothing of the momentum of, say, the 'arms race' of the great nations in it. It is depressing to think that fifty to a hundred times as much money is spent on defence budgets as on development in needy countries in a world where the most significant phenomenon is that poor nations are growing poorer while wealthy ones grow wealthier.

MONSEFU, DECEMBER 1964

"Will you say a Mass of Envy for me, Father?"

He was from Jaen, far up in the mountains, and his eyes glowed with fever. He explained that he had never heard

147

of a Mass of Envy before, but the *brujo* who was curing him had sent him to me to have two Masses offered, one for the intention of restoring him to health, the other to bring misfortune on the friend who was putting poison in his soup. I reasoned with him but am not sure that I was able to counteract the diagnosis. What moved me most, apart from the sadness of it, was curiosity and, when he told me that the man in charge of his curing was Tomas Tullume, a certain wry amusement. Apparently Tomas is anxious to establish a mutual benefit society, sharing profits with us.

What can one do with an illiterate and a-moral witch doctor who, during 'Operation DIG', when the old irrigation ditch was being filled in, was found to be very helpful? When he found that, even without his help, we could call out a hundred and fifty workers on successive Monday mornings, he brought in an extra hundred volunteers to finish the job — and that in spite of the fact that we had denied him all religious privileges, such as being '*padrino*' at a christening.

There and then I decided that in future I would avoid tasting the soup his second wife prepares — even though I appreciated it on other occasions during *minga* work parties.

Our clinic is the best answer to the activities of the *brujos*. There for a fee of one sol (four cents) anyone in need may be treated by the best medical men in Chiclayo who come as volunteers to serve in it. I am happy to report that five drug companies in Montreal have donated two thousand dollars worth of medical supplies of the kind we most need and other contributions have come, unsolicited, from New York and St. John's.

MONSEFU, JANUARY 2, 1965

Front page Christmas news in Peru this year was that the statue of the Infant Jesus was stolen from the Crib in Mocupe church. The papers either did not have the full story or were reluctant to print it. The startling fact is that our friend and former confrère, Father Paul Mooney, was ac-

148

cused of the theft and denounced to the police by the men in charge of the Feast celebration. As a result — and to the embarrassment of the good people of the town who had no part in this affair — his little two-room presbytery was searched before the charge was dropped.

All this was only the flowering of a budding resentment on the part of the organizers of celebrations. They had been making door-to-door collections to raise money for this purpose against an appeal by Father Paul for funds for a major and sadly needed repair job on the interior of the church. Small wonder that he thought this was more important than that the image of the Child of the Manger should be brought through the streets in a midnight procession that would inevitably end in a drunken orgy. The fact is that these men were so inebriated during the Christmas feast procession that they probably lost the statue themselves.

The storm broke on St. Stephen's Day in a mob scene that might have come out of Hollywood. The affair ended when the townspeople came to Father Paul and begged him to remain among them. They claimed that the need of the many should prevail over the greed of the few who, they said, 'would build houses for themselves' from the profits of the feasts. So now all is quiet again in Mocupe and Father Paul is still in there pitching.

For the past several months there have been eight Peace Corps volunteers working in Chiclayo and in the fishing village of San Jose, but so far we haven't had much contact with them. We have a new friend in Dr. Humberto Boggiano who has recently completed a year of service in the Montreal Children's Hospital in Canada and has now joined forces with Dr. Ricardo Ramirez-Gaston in efforts to improve local health conditions. Dr. Ricardo whose home and office are in Chiclayo is planning to spend most of the month of his holidays here in Monsefú, making a study of vital statistics, with particular reference to the families who live along the borders of the polluted irrigation canal. The Monsefú irrigation system receives all the industrial and domestic waste of Hacienda Pomalca, a few miles to the north of us, and it is a proven fact that among the fifteen thousand workers on that great commercial farm the incidence of polio and infectious hepatitis is higher than in any other part of the whole Chiclayo region. It seems likely that Dr. Ricardo's research will reveal related conditions and a higher incidence of intestinal and parasitic diseases than in any of the other towns around. If Monsefú could be declared an emergency zone the government might be persuaded to place the area on a priority list for sanitation. According to present listed priorities, it will be twelve years before that service can be hoped for.

Pomalca did nothing about its pollution problem even after a 'Supreme Decree' was issued a few months ago by the president of the Republic, commanding the owners either to treat their sewage chemically or to build a fifteen mile pipe to the sea to carry it away. The four-months' time-limit expired two months ago, but the problem hasn't even been touched. The people of Monsefú are now ready to close by force the irrigation ditches of Pomalca which bring so much danger and disease to this community. It is unfortunate that the president does not have the support in the two Houses of a majority of the deputies and senators, and so his decrees are not worth much. One of the two strongest opposition parties in Congress is led by one Julio de la Piedra who is a member of the family which owns Pomalca. It will be an interesting fight, but I am not involved. This is right because, as a priest and a foreigner, I shouldn't be in on this. I am no longer mayor and this month saw the end of my term as president of the local Development Junta. Just the same, non-involvement does not mean that I am not interested. I have, fortunately, been able to get expert advice for the people who *are* involved. It is a long step forward if they know what has to be done to better the situation.

Today four Sisters of the Holy Family of Nazareth passed through Monsefú on their way to Santa Cruz in the mountains where the priests from Bridgeport are working. The tally of North American priests and religious in the diocese of Chiclayo is now impressive. There are eleven priests and twenty-three religious, counting Sisters M. Aquin and M. Carmelita who are soon to come from Newfoundland. Much as they may be needed on the home front, no one who is aware of local conditions here could possibly begrudge this help to Peru.

There are many problems involved in having help come from North America. One is that of placement. If the only consideration were to find the right place for the right person or the right team so that the diocese would be best served, this would not be a problem at all. But the human element has to be considered and wisdom must be tempered by justice and charity towards those who may already be working in this area. Sometimes these people are less effective than could be wished through poor training, unfavourable economic circumstances and other adverse factors that are no fault of theirs.

Another problem concerns those who come to help. It has to do with the capacity to feel at home in the way of thinking and living of the people of the country and to understand them without constant comparison with the way things are done at home. This is particularly hard for people who come from well organized communities in highly developed countries.

The other day a friend of mine, a Spanish Vincentian, and I got into a discussion about Christmas customs. We agreed that Christmas below the equator is so different from Christmas in the north that the imagination cannot easily bridge the gap. He told me that when he first came to Peru he trained a choir to sing Christmas carols and it was only after some time that he realised how ridiculous it was to have his choristers, with perspiration streaming down their faces, singing about the winter snow and how cold it was in Bethlehem on that first Christmas night.

The real heat comes usually after Christmas and it hasn't hit us yet; still, there are moments when any movement of mind or body seems unwise. At such times the only cure is the beach and the sea breeze and the tumbling surf.

I've had ten days in Lima, attending a very interesting Pastoral Week Conference, running around to a hundred government offices and meeting the two new Mercy nuns from Newfoundland. The main objective of the running around was to get the Health Department to enforce the decree issued more than six months ago, prohibiting the Pomalca Hacienda from letting its industrial and domestic waste flow into the Monsefú *acequia*. Politically it is a hot potato because of the economic power of the de la Piedra family, linked with the fact that they control one of the three strongest political parties. But, as the Health Minister assured me today, it seems that all forces of heaven and earth are lining up against the Hacienda on this issue.

In spite of busy days I have seen some old friends, and the overpowering heat has not prevented our getting together. Mike Crowley should be back in Peru next month and with him will be a team of five priests from Cork, with a community of nuns to follow. They would like to work on the coast, but there are complex reasons, mostly concerned with national pride, that make for difficulties. It seems a pity that their placement where they could do the most good should be blocked, but I have only a feeble hope that they will be in the Chiclayo diocese.

I am writing this at the airport while waiting for the call to board the plane for Chiclayo.

CAJAMARCA, FEBRUARY 5TH, 1965

My fingers are cold and I find it hard to write. I am high up in the mountains where I am attending another Pastoral Week Conference. I have brought two of my parishioners with me, Miguel Gonzales who has many of the qualities of a community leader and Rosa Elena Sanchez, the most intelligent and active member of the Legion of Mary in Monsefú and a student at the Normal School. They are both getting a great deal out of the course, as am I. It may look self-indulgent to take time off from parish duties so soon after the conference in Lima, but I feel that at this stage in the new reformation of the Church time out for study is not likely to be time wasted.

The course is being given by Father Carlos Alverez Calderes who is the best-informed in the country on pastoral development around the world and on the possibilities here in Peru. I've got so much to discuss now with my companions that we would almost need to have a Pastoral Week of our own to thrash it all out.

I am enjoying the informality of the gathering here. Bishop Dammert has found ways and means of fitting a big crowd into the old bishop's house and mingles with us inconspicuously, making everyone feel at ease. In spite of the fact that his diocese is a very poor one — or perhaps because of it — he is very progressive in spirit, doing all he can to combat illiteracy and the kind of crushing poverty that can be matched nowhere on earth, except perhaps in India. In the parishes of the poor dioceses the priests must either share the poverty of the people or extort from them — a choice that ennobles or shames the one who makes it, but that offers no easy compromise.

Cajamarca lies in a beautiful valley behind the first ridge of the Andes in a climb of about seventy miles in steady ascent from the sea. Nearly all these mountains are barren, with straggling thorn bushes and scrub cactus clinging to the rose or copper-coloured rock-faces. Below, in the little valleys that lead to the sea, all shades of green are spread out. Sometimes irrigation ditches cut across a mountain-face, turning everything below them to lush green, in surprising contrast to the bare cliffs above.

The air is cold up here, and it rains frequently. Children as well as grown-ups wear home-woven blankets called *ponchos*. Usually the faces are disfigured from malnutrition and hard conditions of living. Since I came up here I realise fully what I suppose I must always have known — that most human beings live, and always through the ages have lived, in captivity to poverty.

The Law of Agrarian Reform is being applied now in Peru. Wherever the government has opened an office, hundreds of *campesinos* can be seen lined up in the street, waiting their turn to apply for long-term purchase of the land they work on. The law is infinitely complex and very imperfect, but it should do something towards relieving the land hunger of the people.

Bishop Dammert helps the *campesinos* with their papers in their efforts to obtain land of their own. There are state agencies in the field of social progress whose function is to help, but their efforts are often disorganized. This diocese has several priest-teams appointed by the bishop to work with lay teams in giving short courses to the *campesinos* on ways and means of bettering themselves.

Cajamarca is one of the few places in Peru where the winds of change can be truly felt and where community development *a la criollo* is taking place. The phrase is not easily translated, but it means according to the particular outlook of the Peruvian. Nearly five hundred years of economic injustice have left their mark on the national character and the sense of inferiority that is ingrained expresses itself in many ways. Now in my fifth year in this ancient country I am watching the beginnings of what may well revolutionize not only the temporal order but also the life of the Church. Cajamarca is not the only place in Peru where community development is taking place. There are others: Puno, Vicos, Huacho, and some small outlying sections of Lima that I know of.

MONSEFU, FEBRUARY 23RD, 1965

When I left Cajamarca I drove to Bambamarca with a group that included three German social workers of the 'Miserior' organization, a welfare agency that works high up in the mountains. It is a project of the German bishops and is supported by the home dioceses out of the millions of marks collected during Lent in the churches in Germany for development projects in needy countries. The rest of the

154

convoy consisted of four Peruvian diocesan priests, and Miguel Gonzales and Elena Sanchez from Monsefú.

The way led up a caracol road which spiralled towards the cold ridges of the mountain range. We stopped for a meal of trout at a restaurant on a high plateau, too wind-swept for trees or any vegetation to grow. The structure was made of cane and sagged crazily at an angle of seventy degrees in places.

We reached Bambamarca before sundown after delaying for three hours in a fruitless attempt to repair the 'Miserior' Volkswagen 1500 which struck a rock, damaging its gear system. The vehicle was finally left with a lone mountain family to guard it, until a truck could be arranged for, to tow it back to Cajamarca, and the group came on in the pick-up truck of the Peruvian priests and in our little Volks-wagen.

I have never in my life seen such beautiful country. Well-cultivated valleys between towering mountains, tall eucalyptus trees marking the borders of roads and fields; here and there lines of rectangular openings in the mountain peaks where the pre-Inca peoples buried their dead. There is no Quechua spoken now in that area and the people show signs of being more Spanish than Indian, but it is a closed culture with little contact with the coast or any part of the outside world.

The priest team consists of three who are about the same age as ourselves. They live in primitive conditions and con-sider themselves fortunate, because in their first year, they were crowded into one rented room. One of them, Father Fernandez, is a very spiritual man, but that does not keep him from being deeply involved in the co-operative move-ment. They are experimenting now with the idea of getting straw for the people's hat-weaving from the Peruvian jungle instead of importing it from Ecuador. It is something our own co-operative in Monsefú might well consider. The pastor, Father Mundaca, is concerned mainly with the schools in the town, while the third, Father Bartolini, is very gifted in dealing with the *campesinos* and spends most of the week out in the *campo* with the indigenous communities, each of which has representatives among the hundred and twenty lay 'missionaries' of the parish. I watched these people at a meeting after Mass on Sunday and was greatly impressed when I heard their discussion on co-operative work and voluntary labour on public projects such as schools in which they have an eager interest. The priests tell me the people send their daughters and other women relatives to the German social workers for short courses and for training in handicrafts.

Unfortunately, the three priests have been able to work this magic on only one half of their parish of forty thousand people. The other twenty thousand are on one or the other of two huge haciendas where the haciendados consider the workers to be Communists. To one of the owners the priests have laid down an ultimatum — that he must obey the law of the land and build a school for his workers (or give them land to build their own school) or else they would never celebrate Mass there. This threat is more effective than might appear to any but those who know the hacienda system and the people who work within it.

Here in Monsefú we have begun the rounds of house-visiting again and we find, as time goes on, more confidence in us and more frankness in the attitude of the people. The period of conflict is practically over and, since Monsefuanos are good tinkers, tailors and craftsmen, given to travelling all over the country, they boast about us all over Peru. Their chief source of pride is the Sisters' school, but they have spread the idea also that we are models of pastoral behaviour. This hasn't embarrassed us yet, but some of the effects are noticeable. For instance, our work uniform of black trousers and white shirt with a red Celtic cross stitched on the pocket has become established among the people as the accepted garb for priests and five hundred such shirts, made in Monsefú, are being worn all along the coast.

156

Last night Father Mike Crowley arrived with Fathers Mike Murphy and Tim Sullivan, veterans all, and all from County Cork. Bishop Lucey is expected in Lima on March 8th. In the meantime he has given them *carte blanche* to choose the place of the apostolate.

I had let the bishops of Chiclayo and Trujillo know what a fine group they might get if they could persuade them to come, but the displacement of Peruvian clergy even for obvious pastoral reasons is hard for them to do. The prelate of Chimbote, half-way between here and Lima, has told the Irishmen that he will back them in whatever they decide to do, and all signs indicate that their place of work will be there. Even though they will be a bit far away, it is a great thing to have them working as a team and in co-operation with us. They went on north this morning but will be back here on their return trip in two or three days' time.

There is a lull in the battle with Pomalca and in the struggle to get water-works for Monsefú. When jet planes roar overhead these days from the Air Force base in Chiclayo, I keep remembering that each one costs the government ten million soles, or four hundred thousand dollars — just twice the amount needed to put a workable water and sewer system in this town. The other day three military jet planes were lost in an accident up the coast but, miraculously, no one was hurt.

Now that the *Senor Cautivo* chapel-hall is no longer needed for school classes, we are thinking of using it as a young people's club in the evenings. We have a TV, given us by Archbishop Skinner, which we seldom use because the programming is so poor, but it would be a great attraction there.

We are expecting the Sisters back from their Newfoundland holiday in about two weeks and are hoping to surprise them by having gravel and even a little asphalt around the school.

The Mercy Sisters got back yesterday from their long holiday in Newfoundland, but they were so weary that they had little heart for talk last night. It had taken them fifteen hours to drive from Lima in equatorial heat and for most of the time under a broiling sun. They had had three punctures on the way and by the time they got here had begun to feel that the day would never come to an end.

An excited crowd had gathered to meet them. The Legion of Mary and the Daughters of Mary had organized a reception but we managed to keep the ceremonies short because of the lateness of the hour and the fatigue of the Sisters. In spite of the ordeal of their journey they looked surprisingly well.

We are hoping now that the priests from Cork will take over the parish of Chepen. The town itself has a population of 25,000, but there are another ten thousand living on haciendas nearby. The present pastor is a very zealous young Peruvian whose work is so fruitful that its very effects produce more work than he and his one curate can handle. He has applied for help from his own archdiocese of Trujillo, but no one is available. And now he feels that if a group from outside could come in and take over it would be the best way to solve the problem since he has neither manpower nor money at his command and his own health is breaking under the strain.

Chepen is something of a commercial centre and has both electricity and a water system. This would mean that the Irish priests could get to work at once without too much worry about the health hazards that plague areas less well provided. It is within two hours' drive of Monsefú and is close to other parishes which are greatly in need of help. These could be added as the group's numbers would increase.

It all looked too good to be true, and so it has proved. When I went to Chepen this afternoon I found Bishop Lucey surrounded by four other Cork men. In deference to the tropic heat he was wearing a sports shirt and made an undistinguished figure, until one looked into the eyes which, under heavy brows, are smiling, shrewd and alert. I was present at the conference that followed, but did not take part in it except to point out that proximity to us in Monsefú would be an advantage to both.

The matter has not been definitely decided yet, but the bishop feels that Chepen is already on its way to salvation and does not need the Irish priests. Moreover, he feels that the people back in Ireland who are supporting them would find it hard to understand why an established parish which is well served by two native priests should be taken on when the need elsewhere is so much greater.

When they left Chepen I accompanied them as far as the crossroads, then doubled back to have supper with the pastor and his assistant and to say some office. Father Fernando Rojas is an outstanding man. Neither he nor his curate really want to leave, but the good of the parish is their first consideration and they feel that they are unable to cope with the very size of their commitment. Bishop Lucey claims that four or five men from outside couldn't hope to do even as much as two devoted native priests who are well orientated and who have a thorough understanding of their people.

The team from Cork would consist at first of only two men, but two more would be added in a few months' time when language studies are completed. A fifth would join them later, a priest now serving with Cardinal Cushing's St. James Society in Lima whose contract will be up this year. In three years' time still another would be added. There will also be four Sisters of Mercy from the Cork diocese, two of whom are nurses, who will stay with our Sisters for a while to learn at first hand about Peru and its people. As projects expand, other dioceses in Ireland, inspired by the example of Cork, may also send priests. There may eventually be an Irish St. James Society, similar to Cardinal Cushing's.

The children are back in school after the long holiday and in the next two weeks will be trained to take part in the liturgy of Holy Week. Since we began celebrating Mass in Spanish we have had more response from the people than usual. Some of our Legion of Mary girls have become real apostles. Towards the end of the summer — winter to you up north — they concentrated on preparing for First Holy Communion more than one hundred children. Since then the children have been coming on their own.

The strongest proof we have that God has given increase to our small efforts comes from the discovery that among the lay apostles people are emerging who are dedicated and disciplined beyond the natural capacity of their environment. Some day we may even have someone canonized! However, our actual hopes are less exalted and do not go beyond vocations to the priesthood, the religious life and the lay apostolate. The priests in Bambamarca, for instance, accomplish tremendous things. They know their people better than anyone from outside ever could and serve them the better for that knowledge.

Bishop Lucey has made his choice of a work site for his priests and nuns. He has accepted all the slums of Trujillo and the forty thousand people who live in them. The pastor, Father Mike Crowley, will be a busy man from now on.

The most interesting local development I have to report is that a producer co-operative in home weaving is about to be established in Monsefú. Government representatives are very interested and will guarantee an unlimited market if the price of the product can be kept low enough to break into the international market, and if the quality can be maintained. They rely on us to organize the co-operative and guide it through its critical first months. The idea is simple, but it will become complicated in practice. Nothing is simple or easy in Peru.

Our efforts to change Lenten customs in our parish continue. This year the various societies who are responsible for organizing the events of each day of Holy Week will see to it that all is in keeping with the solemnity of the occasion. Classical and religious music will be played over the loudspeakers in the public square and local bands with flutes and muted cornets will play the sad music of the Passion.

Traditionally, Monsefú has entered Holy Week more in carnival than in religious spirit. This year the Palm Sunday brotherhood will postpone its procession to Easter Sunday when, with their own special statue robed in the sash of victory, they will portray the Risen Christ and the joy of Easter-tide. The brotherhood in charge of Holy Monday proceedings, chastened by last year's cancellation of their procession, has undertaken to observe the spirit of Holy Week. No decision has yet been made as to what to do about the Palm Sunday brotherhood's donkey whose trappings are newer and finer than the vestments of either the statue or the priest. There must be some way of giving him his moment of glory, even though the Palm Sunday procession will not be held. I am reminded of Chesterton's lovely poem about that humble creature:

> ". . . The tattered outlaw of the earth,
>   Of ancient crooked will;
> Starve, scourge, deride me; I am dumb,
>   I keep my secret still.
> Fools! For I also had my hour;
>   One far fierce hour and sweet.
> There was a shout about my ears,
>   And palms before my feet."

I have had it in mind for some time to take a course or two at the newly established University of Lambayeque in Chiclayo, partly because I am interested but also because I think it is a good idea to learn what goes on in an environment where Communism seems to flourish. Today is the second day of classes but the University Federation of Lambayeque, a Communist organization, has taken over the university building. The members have barricaded them-

161

selves inside as a protest against something or other, although no one seems to know just what, and most of the professors have resigned.

Policemen watch from a distance but do nothing. It seems that the autonomy of universities in Latin America is so highly respected that they are permitted to destroy themselves or do grievous harm to the country before there can be any intervention by the forces of law and order. The University of San Marcos in Lima, the oldest in the New World, is in a perpetual state of chaos. Yet, in spite of adverse conditions, many people emerge from the hurly-burly with an education.

During the holidays two sociology students came to Monsefú to do some research preparatory to writing a thesis. I suspect they are Communist in ideology, but I found them very co-operative. University Communists in Latin America don't really know what they are as a rule — except that they are rebels against injustice and exploitation.

These two were doing a statistical study on local products, local skills and, unhappily, on local business mores. Over a period of four months they collected data on milk production, alfalfa and vegetable farming as well as on weaving, carpentering, tailoring, and the making of home brew, chicha. Their professor, a French economist by the name of Collin, asserted that Monsefú, in spite of its humble appearance and squalor, is a great city in microcosm where, in the battle for survival, no holds are barred. The people, he said, are intelligent, industrious — and in general have no standard of honesty.

The research brought out some appalling facts: hardly a drop of milk of the ten thousand gallons distributed from the Monsefú area daily is left undiluted. Some of the 'dairymen' manufacture their product out of the packages of powdered milk they buy for a pittance from the poor families who receive U.S. surplus food through the parish but who, in spite of being told, do not seem to be aware of its nutritive value. Other *entrepreneurs* make pepper out of dust with a little dye added; others use counterfeit wrappers to disguise a product in imitation of a sweet cake associated

162

with the town of Lambayeque. Dr. Collin's students still have three months left before they turn in their report which, they say, will probably be published.

Bill Cotner is a Peace Corps worker from Philadelphia who is helping us every Thursday in our efforts to build the slow educational foundation for the establishment of a marketing co-operative for handicrafts. His judgment is sound and his enthusiasm heartening. We want to make sure this time that responsibility is accepted by the members from the beginning, even though we know that an authentic co-operative will be hard to establish in our Monsefú environment — as Dr. Collin and our own experience would seem to indicate.

Our public works program is progressing, with the Monday *mingas* giving impressive results. Yesterday, during a session, with a bulldozer growling over my shoulder, I used all kinds of persuasion to get an elderly lady to give up part of her yard to our new avenue project. When appeals to civic pride failed I stooped low and reminded her how often I had come to her home with a volunteer doctor to attend her daughter who was paralysed. So then it became a matter of bargaining. She asked me if I would come and put holy oils on her statue of Our Risen Lord. I said he wasn't at all in need of it. After a little further argument we settled for holy water and a new fence.

The avenue over the bed of the former irrigation ditch has been given a width of eighty feet for its whole half-mile length by the neighbours on both sides of it. It has been levelled and covered with gravel and is already in use. It will look better later when trees are planted on both sides.

One of the families owned a field that had to be cut

163

through to smooth a sharp curve. They have donated for a playground one half of the triangle of land left on the town side and now Monsefuanos resident in Chiclayo are planning to get swings and other playground equipment to put there.

Already the people are talking about naming the new avenue and among the proposals are 'Avenue of the Republic of Canada' and 'Avenue of Archbishop Skinner'. I keep telling them that our motive in fostering the project is based on our desire to show them what they can do by their own efforts. I propose that it should be called 'Avenida El Pueblo' to remind them always that the people had done this themselves out of their own good will. Besides, 'El Pueblo' was the name of the former irrigation ditch. I am sure His Grace won't object, nor will 'The Republic of Canada'.*

MONSEFU, AUGUST 10TH, 1965

Last evening as I was walking along the street, I saw an old man sitting on the sidewalk, huddled against a pole. He was protected against the damp chill by a greasy overcoat which he pulled closely around him. The cold Antarctic current which brings fish in abundance to the shores of Peru brings also a winter chill which blows in from the coast at this time of year. It was late, so I asked the old fellow if he were ill. He answered, "No." When I asked if he could use a little money, "I don't need any, thanks," he replied courteously, and seemed just to want to get to sleep unmolested.

It is at such a moment that a foreigner feels repentant if he has ever expressed a low opinion of the natives. There is a certain dignity in them that shows, through ignorance, through poverty, through the very character defects that have grown out of centuries of humiliation. They are a people with a great past and every now and again one gets the impression that some dim memory still remains of a time when this land was really their own.

---

* By decree of the Council after Father Conroy's death, the avenue was given the name, *Avenida Carlos O'N Conroy*.

164

I moved on, remembering another moment not very long ago, when I visited the Little Brothers of Jesus who live and work in one of the worst slums of Lima. Although they do manual work and take jobs in factories to support themselves and their undertakings, they are all either priests or brothers, consecrated by religious vows. They are members of a world-wide Order which has the personal approval of the Pope. Brother John, the Superior for all South America, (although that is not a word they use — they prefer the phrase, 'the one responsible') gave me his thoughts about Peruvians. "They are a wonderful people," he said. "If my own country, France, had been subjected to the same religious history, there would long ago have been nothing left of the Faith." He went on to say that there was much to build on in the Peruvian religious tradition, particularly in the people's deep and sincere devotion to the Cross. We would throw away an advantage, he claimed, if we did not try to nurture the seeds of faith which are to be found in the various brotherhoods who organize the fiestas — even though we might deplore their methods of expressing their devotion. His blue eyes sparkled as he strained to communicate to me what his years of working shoulder to shoulder with Peru's abandoned poor had taught him. By getting to know people truly, he asserted, one gets to see the treasures Our Lord has hidden in humble hearts. I didn't tell him about Dr. Collin.

I was sorry I did not have a tape recorder to take down what he said. His optimism was contagious, and I left the clean little hut, which looked on the outside like all the other hovels by the edge of the Rimac, with a new hope for the future of the Church in Peru. The next time I hear rockets sounding for a fiesta during Mass, I'll think of Brother John's words and will try to regard the explosions as punctuation marks. Usually the brass band hired for the occasion arrives at the church 'in full voice' just at sermon time, escorting the 'padrinos' of the feast in great solemnity. Then one hears the ascending 'swish' of a rocket, and there is a moment for preparing a sentence. Then the bangs begin and

165

the babies all howl vociferously. Sometimes I think they have more sense about these things than their parents.

Ever since early June armed bandits have been making raids up in the mountains. It is rumoured that several thousand men have dedicated themselves to guerilla warfare in the heart of the Peruvian sierra, between Ayacucho and Cuzco, the ancient Inca capital. Property has been destroyed and bridges blown up. Last week a guerilla band killed three policemen who were searching for them. Now, it is not the police, but army rangers, trained in guerilla tactics, who form the search bands. It is very likely that Peruvian Communists, inspired by the anti-U.S. feeling which spread through Latin America, following the United States' intervention in the affairs of the Dominican Republic, decided to try out prematurely their ever-ready plan for revolution. They have only a ghost of a chance this time, but there is good reason for thinking that the explosion will come within the next ten or twenty years — and then it will be a real revolution with every chance of success, whether Communist-inspired or not.

The fate of Peru will be tied in with events in other countries in South America. In the present crisis all known Communist leaders are being jailed. Luis Angel, popularly known by his pen name of 'Sophocles' is among those rounded up. He is the finest humorist in the country and uses sarcasm as a powerful weapon. It is one which has landed him in jail more than once. Many people feel that his sudden silence at this time can do more harm to the government than ever his barbed wit did. Most of the others held in safekeeping never will be missed.

Quite apart from organized revolutionary efforts, there is a spirit of unrest in this country. A few days ago some Young Christian Democrats demonstrated their disapproval of an extravagant party in a luxurious Lima hotel by tossing a bomb into the lobby. It emphasized their point, but violence breeds violence, and I am wondering where all this will end.

166

Events have moved rapidly in the past two or three weeks. It looks as though real trouble has come to Peru, the extent of which cannot be estimated. Armed rebels in the mountains have killed large numbers of police. The military authorities do not allow full coverage of news, claiming it would interfere with their own tactical movements. The country generally is uneasy and rumours are about that 'Che' Guevara who is everywhere regarded as the brain behind Castro's guerilla-type warfare in Cuba, is now in Peru, organizing subversion and revolution. There has even been a declaration of independence in Pucuta, an isolated mountain area that is in close communication with the jungle people. It is apparent now that the June outbreak of guerilla activity was not spontaneous, but was Communist-inspired in Lima.

Through all the flying rumours life goes on as usual. The other day as I sat outside the door of the chapel in our neighbouring fishing village of Santa Rosa, waiting for the key to be fetched, I watched with amusement some little girls who were playing hopscotch in the dusty sand. Children seem to play the same games the world over, but sometimes with a difference. Each of these small ones, as she hopped merrily from square to square, carried a baby brother securely fastened to her back. One infant who was over a year old showed keen interest in the game. Another slept soundly, head lolling, as he was jounced up and down.

We had come to Santa Rosa for First Confessions of children and for confessions of children generally. It is impossible to arrange any regular schedule for two good reasons. For one thing we are too few in number to be able to cope with the full needs of the thousands of people in our parish and for another, the faith has to be awakened and nourished before the sacraments can become effective, so that the approach is slow. We are hoping to have extra help soon in Santa Rosa from a Passionist Father who will be stationed in Pimentel, three miles away, where he is building a seminary for the Order. The distance is about the same as from

Monsefú, but the road between is asphalted and bus service makes communication easy.

Now that September is close at hand, our town is getting ready for the great annual patronal feast. We have had no success whatever in convincing the people that brass bands and fireworks are less important than more permanent values such as building better homes; working for community projects; aiming at better education for their children. They look at us with patient understanding, knowing that it will take us a long time indeed to learn that life without braying band music, exploding rockets, chicha and *marineras*, would be dull and miserable and altogether insupportable.

Before I close, a word about Sister Mary Dorothy, Superior of the Mercy Sisters' Community. How she, in spite of ill health, continues in the circuit of the government schools, catechising all day long, hour after hour, is beyond my understanding. She and Sister Mary Aquin have the hardest of all the jobs, struggling to keep the attention of about two thousand children in the course of a week. They go from one poky little classroom to another, helping teachers whose own knowledge of the faith is little better than that of their pupils. The work is hard, but is just as necessary as the more specialised efforts of the parish school. There must be times, however, when weariness begets discouragement and only dedication can restore the balance.*

MONSEFU, OCTOBER 2, 1965

Now that September is over and with it the feast celebration of Our Lord in Chains, represented by the ancient, beautiful statue which is the most venerated possession of the parish, we can begin to breathe again.

The feast occasion brings strange offerings — among them *ex voto* images wrought in imitation silver which are hung

---

* These are the two sisters who were killed in the same accident as Father Conroy.

on the statue. These may depict human forms kneeling in prayer; farm animals such as oxen or goats; crops of various kinds; sometimes parts of the human body. This year a solid gold heart, with the donor's name engraved on it, surrounded by pearls, was presented. It was not easy for us to bless the devotion of the giver, nor even to thank him for so valuable a gift. It had been made from a *huaco* or ancient tomb artifact dating back over a thousand years and made of pure, unalloyed gold. It was a product of the old Mochica culture which pre-dated the Inca civilization destroyed by the Spaniards. It came from the coastal part of Peru which is still rich in archeological remains. Its value in the eyes of an archeologist would be beyond price, but in its present form even the commercial value of the gold could not be realised, for it would wound the feelings of the people to show so little respect for such an offering.

Among other offerings made is a pair of African doves brought from Sullana by a friend of *El Senor Cautivo*. Before we could make a cage for them they made a nest under our water tank and settled in as part of the family.

After the fiesta was over the parish was the richer in money offerings by about two thousand dollars — gifts from people who came from far and near to prove their devotion to the statue of Our Lord in his representation as a captive. This money is practically the only parish income for the year. And so we thank Our Captive Lord for being good to us during the weeks of His feast celebration. We are half blind from lack of sleep and half deaf from the sound of rockets and brass bands, but we feel that He has treated us well indeed.

News had reached us that Victor had died, but the report proved to be exaggerated — it was his cousin who had passed away. During the September feast he turned up, wispy and bright-eyed as ever, eager to take charge of the candle-wax during the celebration. He is a mischievous old man of seventy who loves to impress people with his 'English' and double-talks to that end. Dressed in his work rags and forage cap he is fearsome to behold. To the Sisters who came to the rescue of a group of children who were being ordered out of his presence he said, "With you they are little angels or little dead flies, but look at what they do when you are not around!"

For ten days Victor protected *El Senor Cautivo* from harm in the hall where hundreds of tallow candles burned. He slept on the floor in his clothes and remained unwashed until he was so black inside and out with the soot of the candles that he looked like one of the chimney-sweeps out of the 'Mary Poppins' movie. Then, on the last day, he accepted a supply of hot water from us, cleaned himself up and appeared again in all his glory to bid us a ceremonial good-bye 'until next year, if God lends us life.' Before he left he and several others helped Father Jim Doody weigh out about two dozen quintals of wax, the remains of the candles left burning before the statue. This had been collected to sell as part of the profits of the feast. Father Jim found that he was the only man who couldn't stand erect in the cramped space beneath the stage of El Senor Cautivo's chapel-hall. Since few people would describe him as a big man, the stature of our average parishioner will have to be imagined.

Our little friend, Porfirio — 'Poppy', as he is generally called, is now four years old. The other day he jumped from a wall, breaking his leg in three places. His father, Fidel, who looks after the parish school, called in a 'sabandero', a local bone specialist, to look after the injury. The splint put on the little leg was made of cardboard and the binding was so tight that it cut off circulation. Only the intervention of the Sisters, the firm decision of Father Jim and the kind and skilled help of our good friend, Dr. Humberto Boggiano, saved the little fellow from losing his leg — or perhaps his life.

We are fortunate in our other medical friends also. Only recently two more have pledged their help. Dr. Carlos Chirinos and Dr. Walter Diaz, young men who as interns in a Chiclayo hospital had come to Monsefú regularly to help in our clinic and who have since completed their internships, have now offered to serve there each week.

We have received word also that a shipment of medical supplies has been sent us from New York by the Catholic Medical Society, and quite recently, through the influence of Monsefuanos living in Lima, a pharmaceutical company there sent us some supplies that were badly needed.

The professional men of Monsefú itself have been less responsive to the parish needs, but we remind ourselves from time to time that interest in community needs is a plant of slow growth. Only recently we have begun to see signs that something good is stirring. I don't think we'll have to wait for Poppy to grow up to find willing helpers in all the various fields of our efforts for our people.

Big changes have come to Monsefú in the past five years. The most encouraging to us is what is happening inside the church. And here I am not referring to the simple beauty of the edifice, but to the spirit and attitude of the people in religious matters. As the years go by young people are coming to church in greater numbers; the *beatas* or nervous-religious have merged into the background of general attendance. We are impressed by the participation of the people in the Mass, both in the prayers that are read and in singing. I have to admit here that this is perhaps due in some measure to the local character. Our parishioners are not sensitive to a neighbour's discomfort, nor would a man consider that his shouted response might prevent someone else from praying.

We are seeing a real growth in respect and attention at Mass, although this sometimes tends to go too far. Only last Sunday a woman almost suffocated a small child who was roaring out his indignation at finding himself in church. In general, the people are beginning to respect the wishes of babies who indicate that they would rather not be present.

One of our parishioners is a bit of a puzzle to us. She is small and anaemic and is about forty years of age. She attends about twenty Masses a week and receives Communion daily. She intones the responses in a slightly cracked voice whether the Mass is high or low. We are at a loss to know whether she should be decorated for her fervour or gagged and bound for interrupting the solemnity of the occasion.

171

She wears no head-covering, and that is an offence to local custom. In these parts it is equivalent to, say, calling at the Vatican wearing bicycle shorts instead of conventional garb. The other day, as she approached the altar rail, an over-zealous visitor from Chiclayo, galvanized by the shock of it, came up behind her with a mantilla, stalking her as if she were a giant moth, and whipped the black net down over head and face. Our heroine fought off the attack peevishly and received Communion as usual.

The work of the Sisters is the most important factor in all the parish developments. Most of their time is given to the parish school, but through the young people they are reaching into every home in one way or another. Other schools are imitating their methods. The people of our thriving big-neighbour town, Chiclayo, look enviously at what is being done for the *cholitos* or mixed-blood country children who, they feel, will walk away with all the prizes.

We are seeing at last in our town the beginnings of the technical progress we have been working for over the past five years. At the entrance to the town the tall water tower which will hold ten thousand gallons of drinking water is almost finished; a medical post which will contain a residence for a doctor and a minute cottage hospital, is being built; three classrooms in the government high school are nearly finished; trenches have been dug through the streets of the town to extend the water system. Next year, we are told, we are to have running water and, it is hoped, a sewage system. With solution of the hygiene problems the need will become more pressing for progress in other fields. We hope to be in the forefront of the town's development, but at the same time to transmit to our people the faith of our fathers and theirs in all its beauty and force.

MONSEFU, NOVEMBER 8, 1965

I am writing this evening from Father Paul Mooney's new four-room presbytery in Mocupe, a town a few miles to the south of Monsefú, where seven of us have gathered for a housewarming. A game of Hearts is in progress but since seven is too many for a good game, I am being permitted to hole up in a corner to write a letter, leaving the others to disport themselves.

It is too soon yet for us to have heard the results of the Latin-American collection at home, but we are hoping that the generosity of the people will make it possible for us to pay off most of the debt on the new classrooms of the parish school.

We ourselves have also been involved in a diocesan Mission collection which has just been completed. A total of eight hundred dollars was brought in in copper coins of the value respectively of one-fifth, two-fifths, four-fifths of a cent, together with larger coins of two and four cents' value. The bulk and weight of that sum would have to be seen to be believed, and I don't like to think of the dismay of the bank teller who will have to count it.

We have good news from Lima. There is every reason to hope that the Government will give us a building subsidy of eight thousand dollars. This amount, together with the money from the September feast, will go far towards building an auditorium for the school which will also be used for the town's needs. We have the assistance of a Peace Corps architect, Nicholas Parakis, who is helping us with the plans. He has already made a scale model for presentation to government officials in Lima for their consideration. He has made a series of sketches as well, illustrating alternative seating arrangements to meet the multiple purposes of the hall. The project will cost only a fraction of the amount that would be required for such an undertaking in Canada or the United States. But this land, so near the Equator, has no extremes of climate. There are no high winds, no driving snow, no rain even, to give the builder any cause for worry.

There are other Peace Corps workers in Monsefú also. Roy Martin, sixty-five years old, is from Georgia. He is an expert in chicken farming who, in spite of difficulty with the Spanish language, delivers good talks over the loud-speaker in the public square. Then there is Mary Ann Raymond from New Jersey who cheerfully endures the hard-

173

ships of Peace Corps life and the discouragement in dealing with the people that is her daily portion. And we are relying on another Peace Corps worker, Bill Cotner, to develop our Straw Products Co-operative which is now well under way. A display of the products has been arranged for Chiclayo in December and for Lima in January in the hope of opening up markets for the work. The members, up to now, have only been making samples for *Artesianas del Peru*, a U.S.-backed agency for promoting handicrafts, but no substantial orders have been received as yet.

Through our Peace Corps workers we have become acquainted with many of their colleagues. There is Ted Collins, a giant of a man, six feet four tall. He is a brainy accountant who is working in an area where there is a strong anti-U.S. feeling; Mike Lyons, who is having some success in organizing a fisheries co-operative in the town of San Jose, north of here; Steve Brush who is trying to organize a chain of co-operatives, with Chiclayo as centre.

Peace Corps training is relentless and demanding and is essentially a course in survival. The trainees are not spared the hard facts of the life they are to face and when they become field workers are prepared to take on difficult — sometimes impossible — jobs. They learn to cope with the loneliness of separation from their own kind and culture and to be patient in dealing with prejudice against their nation and people. They all come to their chosen country equipped with useful skills which they are eager to share. What the training cannot do for them, however, in the few months they are with it, is to give them an insight into the people they are to serve — nor can it provide them with a plan of work which will make them generally effective. And not always can they get enough of a new language for full communication with the people they are to live among. Theirs is no easy task, and it is not surprising that they are not always successful. Two years, the term of their service, is too short a time for any deep understanding of a people whose way of thinking is centuries removed from them.

In our area of northern Peru, there is a special complication for, behind the Spanish front (which is something of

174

an enigma anyway to the practical North American) lies
the Indian mind, uncommunicative at best, misleading always in its manner of expression.

It seems to be the fate of the Americans that they should
have to face failure in so many of their undertakings, in
spite of their great resources both in material things and in
dedicated people. That the Peace Corps, in spite of its ad-
mirable ideals, shares this failure is substantially evident
in Peru.

The Sisters continue to lead a busy life and to win the
respect and affection of the people. But in this regard, as
always in human relations, distinctions are made — as with
Don Manuel in Calanca. Every Sunday this blind old man
with his wife and daughters gets a ride to the Mass held in
the country chapel, seven miles from Monsefú. And every
Sunday he gratefully kisses the hands that help him; but it
is only when Sister M. Gabriella is along that he is eager to
pay the four cents for the taxi ride. I need hardly add that
as a result she is much teased by her companions.

There is little further to report. Tomorrow will be a busy
day and will be spent on the church land, assisting with
arrangements for transfer to tenant farmers and getting involved in the red tape of legal technicalities.

MONSEFU, DECEMBER 3, 1965

The days are very full with many and varied tasks. Today
I am off to Chiclayo in search of a volunteer dump-truck
for use in next Monday's *minga*. While there I must arrange
about new tax forms in connection with the parish land;
confer with a lawyer about getting possession of a property
on the other side of the Church Square — won in the Supreme Court against the Town Council seven years ago,
but never claimed for the parish; arrange with a theatre
owner to have our school Christmas concert put on in
Chiclayo, and have tickets and a programme printed; pick
up samples of the craft work of our Straw Co-operative for
the December Display in Chiclayo; attend to some business

175

for the Santa Cruz priests who are high up in the mountains, prevented by impassable roads from getting down to the coast for any but urgent reasons.

Father Jim and Father John are spending a day of recollection at the Convent, following a strenuous programme with the First Communion classes of the two biggest schools for girls in Monsefú. The final examinations preceding the long 'summer' holidays are now being held. When school is over our young First Communicants will scarcely see the inside of a church again until classes assemble in three months' time. Lack of concern about Sunday Mass is common in all Latin America. The people do not accept the Church's ruling as a matter of duty and discipline as we do in our Irish way at home — although our feeling about the Mass goes much deeper than that. At any rate, we have visible proof in the increased attendance, particularly of the young adults, that the situation is growing better. Just the same, ours is no runaway victory — and we have visible proof of that too. Last Sunday I went over to give Communion to a man who summoned me just as I was returning to the altar, only to find that what he wanted was a blessing on some holy pictures. And it isn't unknown for a late-comer at Mass to tap the celebrant on the shoulder just at the moment of the Consecration to ask for holy water.

I am happy to report that our parish school won a trophy in the Chiclayo Music Festival. It was given in a competition between school choirs in a television performance. Our children are first in their category, one among four winners.

We have news at last that the Government will give us a grant of eight thousand dollars for the auditorium. It is a definite promise, because the Budget Committee has approved the amount and the politicians have stated publicly that it is to be for a parish civic centre.

MONSEFU, DECEMBER 21st., 1965

Father Mike Crowley came up from Trujillo yesterday and stayed with us overnight. For the best part of a year now he and his four confrères from County Cork have been struggling with appalling conditions in the *barriadas* or slums of Trujillo which is one of the four largest cities in Peru. They could have chosen an easier assignment and still have done good work — but they are Irishmen and we all know that the Irish are ever ready to meet a challenge. The *barriadas* of Trujillo are without light, running water or sewerage. When the Cork men went there, there was no church, or presbytery, no convent — but there were forty thousand people living in desperate poverty and pitiably in need of help. Now, less than a year later, the place is humming with activity. The little band of priests did not wait for good things to happen; they *made* them happen — with strong support from their home diocese of Cork. They are building not one, but two presbyteries, strategically located where they will best serve the people; also a convent, a school and a church. And, inspired by their leadership, the people themselves have managed to obtain over a mile of water-pipe which is being laid by volunteer workers, street by street. In spite of the magnitude of the undertaking and the speed of accomplishment, nothing is being done that is not carefully thought out, planned and agreed upon beforehand.

Father Mike brought with him the latest issue of an Irish publication, 'The Yule Log', containing a collection of stories, poems, articles, puzzles, games for Christmas, etc. This particular issue was of great interest to us, for it had an article on St. John's, Newfoundland, in it. The author claims that city to be the most Irish in North America, although few in Ireland are aware of it. The writer states that Daniel O'Connell was fighting as much for the Irish in Newfoundland as for those at home, and that he helped Bishop Fleming get the land grant for the present Basilica. He tells also of how the stone for the great church that would enable six thousand people to attend Mass at the same time, was brought out, load by load, in sailing vessels, serving as ballast. The same vessels would return with cargoes of fish from the abundant shores of the great island. It is strange that the happenings of over a century ago should still be a living memory in a small corner of Ireland.

This evening we are entertaining in Chiclayo several doctors and others who have been helping us in our parish dispensary during the year. They are Dr. Carlos Chirinos and Dr. Walter Diaz who each come once a week, with Carlos' fiancée who is an excellent nurse and has the full confidence and warm affection of the people; Dr. Ricardo and his wife and Dr. and Mrs. Boggiano will also be with us.

Before leaving for Chiclayo and a happy evening with friends, I am to give a talk to a group who are preparing for marriage. I have a particular interest in one wedding that is to be celebrated tomorrow, that of Carlos J. Llontop, aged sixty-five, and his bride of fifty-five. He has been thinking it over for the past several years and has finally decided that tomorrow, on his birthday, it would be the right thing to do. His twelve children and a number of his grandchildren will be the only guests.

Carlos has been a strong supporter of ours for a long time and, as the owner of the local paper, 'Claridades', has been public in his approval of our doings. About three years ago, however, he resigned from a religious society rather than regularise his marriage. I suppose he thinks such a fine thing as marriage deserves long preparation. I don't think he would be ready yet to take on the heavy responsibilities of that state if his children had not kept on urging him.

Our African doves are three in number now, and a fourth will soon be pecking its way out of its shell. They adopted us on sight, as soon as they were presented to us during the September fiesta and since then they have had the full run of the house. They are so silent most of the time that one never knows when or from what corner one is being observed.

MONSEFU, DECEMBER 28TH, 1965

This is the day of the Holy Innocents and in Latin-American folklore, the day for the *vivos* to trick the *zonzos*. No

178

one trusts anyone on this day of the year and it wouldn't surprise me if the bank refused to cash a cheque.

The closing exercises of the parish school before the long vacation were held about ten days ago. A couple of days earlier we went off to the beach with one bus-load and three buslet-loads of children — a reward for their good showing in the exams and concerts at the end of the year. In spite of the large numbers of children, there was no great danger of anyone drowing as they are afraid of the water where it crashes although they enjoy it where it laps lazily along the shore-line. Father Jim is in charge of the school, but he didn't look very authoritative that day when he was buried in wet sand and splashed with sea-water by the youngsters. And when it came to wrestling he set quite a few of the boys rolling.

We all had a lunch prepared by the Sisters. Then the outing ended in a fishpond in which all received prizes. In spite of the fatigue of preparing examinations, training the children for several concerts — one senior, one junior and a small one given by the Sunday School children, the nuns took time out to plan and supervise this day at the beach. Now that school is out they will enjoy a brief respite, but this year they will stay in Monsefú during the long vacation, and I have no doubt they will be able to intensify their influence for good on the parish and on the people.

As I looked at the youngsters frolicking on the beach that day, celebrating the close of another school year, I realised more than ever how important it was going to be that we should keep in touch with the older boys who are now within one year of high school. We fully intend to keep them in the parish school, however we manage it, because the local school system is so pitiful in quality that if we abandon them to it in their adolescent years all the value of what has been done for them will be lost. What we need now is a high school that will also be a parish school, but our own archdiocese cannot be asked to take on so heavy an obligation. We have already asked for and been given a twelve classroom school as well as a presbytery, while the convents of the Mercy Order in Newfoundland have come forward and shouldered the cost of the Sisters' convent here.

We are beginning to feel a little optimism about the Peruvian government's interest in our work. When I was in Lima in November to appeal for help in building a civic centre, I also looked into the possibility of a school grant which would enable us to add more classrooms to the parish school and, since the decree of the government that lay teachers in schools under parish administration might be paid by the state, I asked also for a grant to pay the salaries of three lay teachers to help the Sisters. With the grant for the civic centre already safely in the budget, I have great hopes that other favours will follow. A truckload of playground equipment has also come to us and this will bring great joy to the youngsters of our parish.

MONSEFU, JANUARY 12, 1966

Our menagerie is growing. A chameleon, looking for all the world like a miniature dinosaur, has taken up residence among the geraniums. A cat got into the store-room where the African doves have made their nest and made a home for herself overnight in a chest of drawers that had one drawer missing. She was obviously intent on establishing a dynasty and was wise enough not to disturb the doves. But all in vain. The storeroom was cleaned out and herself among the unwanted items. Cats down here are wild creatures, as are dogs. The Sisters were given a pup last month to serve as a watchman and he's a scandal in the community – white and fluffy from frequent bathing, and perfumed with talcum powder as no respectable canine should be. He is called 'Newfy' and the curve of his mouth turns up in a sardonic grin which clearly says, "I'm getting away with murder, but I'm not admitting anything."

A few days ago I had my first look at the Peruvian jungle. Bellavista, on the Huallaga river, is about three hundred miles inland and can be reached from the coast only by air. I travelled in a C-130 Hercules transport plane belonging to

180

the U.S. Air Force, one of the two sent from Panama to air-lift road construction equipment to that area.

There is an abundance of coconut palms, chirimoya and other tropical vegetation there. The river flows swiftly but muddily and is the principal means of transport. Dug-out canoes and the crudest form of rafts, loaded with bananas and bundles of heavily-salted river fish, moved constantly along that swiftly-flowing highway. In the three hours I spent there I found it most interesting to observe the life of the place. There was continuous going and coming to and from the grassy river bank, to wash clothes or to fill jars with water which were then transported on the heads of the water-carriers. The people are less obviously Indian than our own coastal people.

The road to be built in the area will be a section of the planned 'margin of the jungle' road connecting Colombia, Ecuador, Peru and Chile along the inside rim of the Andes where the hills are low and the heat bearable. The USAF personnel and the Peruvian captain in charge of the operation in this area are fine people, efficient and friendly. The Hercules plane is a wonder and, with a full gas load, can carry items such as dump-trucks, front-end loaders, steam-rollers run by diesel fuel, tank-trucks, bulldozers and graders — up to fifteen tons weight.

This morning, Sunday, after first Mass, Father Jim flew off to the jungle in the Hercules, as I had done on Friday, but was back in time to be the celebrant of the 6 p.m. Mass. As I write, the quaint thought occurs to me that if the pilot of the great transport plane could command a time-machine to take him back to the remote past to study the transport ways of an ancient world and a vanished civilization, he would probably see no more than Father Jim and I saw as we separately stood on the grassy bank of the Huallaga and watched the river traffic of that remote jungle village go by.

CAJAMARCA, JANUARY 27TH, 1966

On Sunday last I was in Bambamarca, beyond reach of civilization, and today I am writing from Cajamarca where, on the 29th day of August in the year 1533 A.D. the last Inca Emperor, Atahualpa, met death at the hands of his Spanish executioners after a mockery of a trial. It is a fact of history that captive kings seldom live long. The writers of the period describe this monarch as being cruel and ruthless but, as the Incas had no written language, history has handed down only what his enemies have said. During the months of his captivity he won the respect and admiration of his captors and met his shameful death with quiet dignity.

Bishop Emmett Carter of the London, Ontario, diocese has recently arrived on a visit to his priests, Fathers Bill Cooney, Paul Mooney, Vince Gleason and Jack Hurley. We have maintained close touch with the London men and are looking forward almost as much as they are to their prelate's visit.

Last week Father Jim Doody and I went down to Cartavio, just north of Trujillo, to attend a farewell meal in honour of Father Tom Curran of the Holy Cross Fathers there. It had been decided among us the evening before that I would take a brief holiday before January 30th when Father John Maddigan is to leave for his annual retreat with the Maryknoll Fathers. So I went off to Trujillo with Father Michael Crowley and the other Irishmen who had come for the occasion. I stayed with them overnight and flew to Cajamarca the next day with Father Michael Reardon, the latest of the Cork men to arrive in Peru. He had been in Africa for three of the five years of his priesthood and this journey over the cold ridges of the mountains was to give him his first impression of the Andes.

We stayed at the *Hotel de Turistas* which is even cleaner and nicer than the similar government hotel in Chiclayo, and went on to Bambamarca by bus the next day. During the seven-hour journey along the spine of the mountain I lay sprawled among the tarpaulined baggage on the roof of the bus, gazing at the breath-taking scenery and taking pictures. Occasionally I dozed, with a foot wedged in the metal catwalk and an arm twined around a rope, while the golden sun spread glory around us.

Our route followed a road eleven to twelve thousand feet high and so rough that even the pictures I took at one five-hundredth of a second may turn out to be blurred.

As we had known beforehand, the three priests of the Bambamarca parish were due to go to Cajamarca to attend the annual pastoral week with their bishop. Father Reardon returned with them the next day which was Sunday, while I stayed on to take the evening Mass. I had forty baptisms that day and five more on Monday before leaving for Cajamarca at mid-day. A busman's holiday, certainly.

I travelled in the same Volkswagen 1500 with the same three German girls who had been in our convoy a year ago when I paid my first visit to Bambamarca, only this time we were going in the other direction. I hoped, in vain as it turned out, that we would have better luck with that vehicle. The work these girls do in the field of adult education among the forty thousand people of the area is little short of miraculous. All three have a wonderful spirit which reminded me of the care-free happiness of the student groups I encountered hiking in Europe many years ago. They live cheerfully on a small budget. *Miserior*, the organization which sent them and which, as I have mentioned before, is under the direction of the bishops of Germany, provided the money for a Centre where short courses could be given to women of the *campo* who would live in. Unfortunately, construction of the building had to be suspended because the parish priest, my friend, Father Bartolini, tried to build too ambitiously, so that the funds were exhausted before the Centre was completed. The courses are being given, nevertheless, but under restricted conditions of comfort and space.

We started off happily at noon on the seven-hour journey. Most of the way the road was like a dry and rocky river-bed — except that the rocks were sharp instead of being rounded by the action and flow of water. When we had our first flat we found that the jack (which had recently been repaired) would not support the weight of the car. We ran it up on a stone, propped it, took out the stone and dug under the wheels — while it rained intermittently. In the rarified air the effort was fatiguing, but we finally managed to get the spare tire on. Some hours later, as we began the descent towards Cajamarca, with ten miles still to go, a second tire went. I rode into town on the top of truck and returned with reinforcements. But it was after midnight before the Volkswagen finally reached Cajamarca.

Experiences like this make a holiday memorable. Happily, in retrospect, the cold and the wet no longer have power to penetrate. Now I am back in the tourist hotel, comfortably appreciative of my surroundings and no longer unhappy as I was at first at the thought of living like a king for a couple of days in the midst of the bleak poverty of the people in the area.

Earlier this month we held a dump-truck *minga* and managed to get a great quantity of gravel spread on our new *avenida,* over the area of the old irrigation canal which was filled in last year. The following day seventeen men turned up to redirect the flow of water from the irrigation ditch near the Convent, draining off the slimy pools that have been a breeding ground for most of the mosquitos that have plagued the nuns and made life miserable for them for a long time. Among the volunteer workers were four men who were jailed a few nights earlier for shouting, "Hurrah for Communism!" in front of the police station. They were drunk, of course, but are the first in the history of Monsefú known to have brought the police out at night.

Connected with the incident just recounted was a visit the next day by a member of the plain-clothes police force who attempted to incriminate Miguel Gonzales, the male teacher in our parish school and our most valuable helper in practically all our projects. It seems the local Town Council suspected him of being the author of a handbill attacking them as incompetents and denounced him to the police as a Communist. Considering the current official uneasiness about Communism and the continuing campaign against Communist terrorists in the hills this was a serious and sinister charge to make. But Miguel doesn't easily flinch and of course this is par for the course in a place where petty jealousies and petty pride are rampant. I protested vigorously, telling the policeman that if he was hunting Communists he was far off the track. I said that I, personally, would be glad to claim Miguel as a brother. The defence rested on that and the accusation was dropped.

MONSEFU, FEBRUARY 15, 1966

The farthermost part of the parish of Monsefú can be reached by travelling five miles along a dusty road on the other side of the Panamerican highway. A cluster of cane houses makes up the village of Alican which nestles around the Cerro San Bartolo, a hill so small that it is little more than an outcrop of rock. It is said that it was the original settlement of the people who, fleeing from the ravages of a virulent epidemic, later founded Monsefú. That was more than five hundred years ago, and not very long before the Spanish conquest of Peru. In all the years that followed, adding up into centuries, Alican remained small, unimportant and poor.

The children of the village of Alican are too far from the nearest school to have any hope of attending and few of them ever had any dream of education until the Sisters from Monsefú arrived on the scene in January of this year. Every day now our Ranchero truck trundles along the dusty road, picking up children as it goes, until it arrives, crowded, at Alican where the main group is waiting. While Father Maddigan goes off to visit the families scattered throughout the area, the Sisters hold classes for seventy or more children. On Saturday afternoon Mass is celebrated in the open air. There is, on occasion, a noticeable lack of formality as, for instance, yesterday when Father John stepped back to genuflect and trod on a cat! The unhappy creature let the fact be known for miles, and Father John was visibly shaken. But what these country Masses lack in solemnity is made up for in the warm appreciation and sincerity of the people who never in their lives before have known such opportunities. They have strong community spirit and deep religious feeling which, though unformed, is genuine and sincere.

185

Valle Hermoso is another part of our parish that is getting special attention since the Sisters decided to devote their holidays to country work. For the past two years the families of this community have been at odds with the government teacher, with the result that only a dozen or so children turn up for classes. This teacher has done her best (or perhaps I should say her worst) to obstruct the building by the people of a new three-room school — even though the government would supply the materials. She has set families one against another and deliberately sowed discord. The few children who attend class appear to have learned nothing from her but bad words. Now, at last, this woman is being moved out although for a long time, because she had married someone in the Education Office in Chiclayo, she managed to hold her job.

Sisters Maura-Clarita and Gabriella have had to work hard with the sixty children of school age in this community to bring them up to any standard at all. For the most part they are bright youngsters and eager to learn. It is encouraging that in just these past few weeks they have learned to read, write, do sums and sing on a true note; and they have learned a little about their religion. We feel that things are coming along very well indeed. Father Doody offers Mass weekly in Valle Hermoso and we are encouraged to find how good the response is.

MONSEFU, FEBRUARY 25TH, 1966

I have just come back from Niepos, having been away from the home base for five days. I went there partly out of curiosity and partly because Bishop Dammert of Cajamarca had asked us to assist him in getting Father Pascual, a Spanish Vincentian, up there to preach a mission. The parish is in the diocese of Cajamarca, but can only be approached from Chiclayo.

Father Pascual comes from Galicia on the northern coast of Spain and from him I learned much about the fishermen who come out to Newfoundland each year from that country. About half the Spanish fishermen who come out are

Basques and the rest Gallegos. The latter speak a Spanish that is closer to Portuguese than to Castilian and have no problem when they meet the crews of the Portuguese White Fleet who are yearly visitors to Newfoundland.

Niepos is a parish that has been without a resident priest for fourteen years, although its boundaries contain about thirty thousand people. It perches on a mountain ridge, about three thousand feet above its nearest neighbour, more than eight thousand feet above Monsefú and perhaps fifty miles from it as a condor would fly — except that condors prefer the rarified air of the heights and like to remain in Niepos. In the old parish house there I saw the remains of a young condor spread out on the wall. Although it hadn't lost the white markings of its early growth, it measured over eight feet from wing-tip to wing-tip.

I came back to Monsefú with a gift *poncho* of home-woven home-dyed wool. It is like a small maroon blanket with a slit in the centre for slipping the head through when it is being worn as a garment. I was also given the skin of an animal that looked like a bobcat but was spotted like a leopard. Father Pascual was presented with the skin of a mountain cat, silvery in colour.

There are deer and an immense variety of flora and fauna in the Niepos area; and a two-hour walk would bring one to pleasant trout country. The neighbouring parish of San Miguel is a twelve-hour journey on horseback from Niepos. That part of the country is even more thickly populated and is now also without a priest. The three-hour journey by pony from the nearest truck point to Niepos itself left me unable to stand upright when I dismounted. The animals move with a steady but very slow pace and, if it were not for the load of baggage and the mud stirred up by the regular afternoon rains of an Andean summer, it would be easier and perhaps quicker to travel on foot.

On the way back when my attention was momentarily distracted while I was taking a picture, my beast took off on a narrow side-path that had no turning. He slipped once before I could dismount to let the young lad who was acting as guide rescue him.

This boy, about fourteen years of age and in first grade in school, is an orphan. He had never been baptised because no one wanted to take any responsibility for him. I encountered him at a place called Naranjo on the way down from the mountain where I tarried to celebrate Mass for the hundred or more people who live there. While I was there I baptised him as well as a baby. He afterwards came with me as guide, circling down the mountain for two hours towards La Florida where I counted on getting a truck back to Chiclayo. As we passed by groves of coffee and bananas I tried to add to his understanding of what had just happened to him by telling him something of the history of the chosen people since Abraham, attempting to put it into terms he would understand. There was a steady accompaniment of "Si, Si," but I didn't really discover how much got through to him. For the last hour I tried to ease things for the pony, as these mountain animals are not very big, so I walked, inviting people who lived by the road to come on down to La Florida for the Mass.

It is the custom in these communities for the public authorities to pass the word along. In La Florida, however, the mayor was on a binge, celebrating the transfer of the Chief of Police, so there was not as good response there as had been in Niepos or Naranjo. The next morning I took the first truck out and found that the mayor was one of the passengers for the fifteen-minute drive down to his house. He apologised, regretting his condition. He had been at it all that night too, but he said he had to say good-bye properly to so excellent an officer. When we stopped at his house a gasoline-drum of raw rum was rolled up on the truck, to be dropped off without ceremony or taxes at Cayalti on the way down. While they were loading I inspected the still and could easily see why the Mayor and the Chief of Police would have to be such good friends.

And now I am back in Monsefú with a backlog of things piled up waiting for attention.*

---

* Before this letter arrived, news had been received of the fatal accident of March 1st.